Toddler Activities **Made Easy**

Toddler Activities

MADE EASY

100+ FUN AND CREATIVE LEARNING ACTIVITIES FOR BUSY PARENTS

Krissy Bonning-Gould

Illustrations by Aviel Basil

ROCKRIDGE
PRESS

Interior and Cover Designer: Suzanne LaGasa
Art Producer: Sue Smith
Editor: Orli Zuravicky
Production Editor: Andrew Yackira
Illustrations: Aviel Basil
Photography © Antonio Gravante/iStock, Cover; © FatCamera/iStock, ii, xii; © Kirbyphoto/iStock, p. 14; © Lisa Penn/Alamy, p. 40; © monkeybusinessimages/iStock, p. 66; © Chihana/Adobe Stock, p. 94; © Melpomenem/iStock, p. 118; © Choreograph/iStock, p. 144.

ISBN: Print 978-1-64152-538-1 | eBook 978-1-64152-539-8

For all of the hardworking parents, caregivers,
and teachers who shape our world through
meaningful connection with children.

Contents

CHAPTER 3: Explore Your World 41

CHAPTER 4: Get Creative 67

CHAPTER 5: Let's Pretend 95

CHAPTER 6: **Outdoor Adventure** 119

Fun in a Flash!

Toddlerhood is a time when children between the ages of one and three years old are brimming with enthusiasm and wonder—and growing rapidly, too! In fact, most toddlers are moving and learning so fast that trying to keep up with them can sometimes feel challenging for parents and caregivers. I've experienced this feeling firsthand throughout my many years as a parent, art teacher, and blogger at B-InspiredMama.com. The good news is I have also discovered that with a little bit of creativity and imagination, you can use everyday household items to create activities that are designed to be fun, hold the attention of your curious little one, and, as an added bonus, help them learn, too!

No-Fuss Playtime

My toddler parenting journey has taken many forms throughout the years. From being a new stay-at-home mom fighting postpartum depression to a tired pregnant mama chasing a toddler, from being a single mom in a tiny apartment to a mom of children with various special needs, each of these experiences came with its own unique challenges. No matter what leg of my journey I was on, I often felt like there was a roadblock keeping me from being the parent my toddlers needed.

It took getting to the other side of toddler parenthood—my kids are now well into childhood and even their tween years (oh my!)—to see that those challenges were not actually roadblocks at all. Throughout those difficult times, I found myself using my creativity from my art-teaching days to repurpose everyday materials for craft projects, play ideas, and learning activities. When I couldn't afford new toys, I came up with a fun way to play with plastic mixing bowls. When I simply couldn't fathom loading the kids up in the car to go to playgroup, I got them moving with an imaginative game at home instead. And when I didn't have the perfect supplies for that toddler craft on Pinterest, I adjusted it by using cotton swabs from the cabinet instead. My perceived limitations inspired more creativity, imagination, and plain old fun in my days with my toddlers. Perhaps more important, all the creative and easy fun we had together strengthened our connection and allowed my toddlers to practice some key early childhood development skills.

Not only were these personally rewarding experiences for me and my children, the value of these types of interactions is backed up by academic study. In fact, the Center on the Developing Child at Harvard University published an article entitled "Serve and Return" that supports the importance of the kind of back-and-forth that takes place between a young child and a parent or caregiver when they do things together. According to the article, "When an infant or young child babbles, gestures, or cries, and an adult responds appropriately with eye contact, words, or a hug, neural connections are built and strengthened in the child's brain that support the development of communication and social skills. Much like a lively game of tennis, volleyball, or Ping-Pong, this back-and-forth is both fun and capacity-building." It turns out that this "serve and return" that my toddlers and I were doing—and what you do with your toddler—is an integral part of early childhood development. And experts agree: simple, authentic, interactive play benefits your toddler regardless of fancy materials, complex steps, or advanced educational concepts.

In this book, I offer more than 100 easy and fun activities for you and your toddler to do together! Each activity calls for an average of five items, most of which you should already have around the house. The majority of these activities require five minutes or less of preparation time, and every activity can be done in under 20 minutes from start to finish. Most also include suggestions for interacting, connecting, and learning with your toddler, offering ways for you to enhance your "serve and return." So don't let materials, time, space, or expense make you doubt your ability to connect with your toddler. Go ahead and start playing!

Toddler Time

Just because the activities in this book are low on materials and low on preparation, doesn't mean they are low on learning! Every busy movement, babbling sound, and distracted thought toddlers have aids in their development. The guide below lists some of the specific skills your toddler will develop between the ages of one and three. Use it to help you decide which activities are right for your child today.

But before we dive in, a quick word of encouragement from a fellow mama and caregiver who's been there: Don't let detailed developmental milestones worry you so much that they get in the way of you having fun with your toddler! I know you've heard it before, but it's worth repeating: All children develop at their own pace and in their own way. Yes, you should absolutely monitor your child's development with the guidance of your pediatrician, but ultimately follow your child's lead and your instincts when choosing what's right for you both, and that includes the activities in this book.

12 to 18 Months

The focus on rapid physical growth throughout infancy begins to slow as babies reach their first birthday and move into toddlerhood. The focus then shifts to how their bodies interact in space and with the world around them while they work on mastering new skills. Here are some specific skills that often start to emerge at this stage.

Gross Motor Skills

- Stands without support
- Walks with few falls
- Squats to pick something up
- Sits independently on a chair
- Climbs stairs or furniture
- Tosses a ball underhand while seated

Fine Motor Skills

- Claps their hands
- Waves goodbye
- Holds a crayon and scribbles
- Uses fingertips to pick up small objects
- Drinks from a cup
- Uses a spoon
- Scoops materials for play
- Stacks a couple of objects
- Bangs objects together

Language and Social-Emotional Skills

- Continues babbling
- May use five to ten words
- Points at familiar people and objects in pictures
- Imitates others during play
- Can identify a couple of body parts
- Shakes their head to respond to yes/no questions
- Follows simple directions
- Has an interest in interacting with people
- Can locate objects that have been pointed to
- Turns their head in response to hearing their name

18 to 24 Months

As toddlers reach their second birthday, social and play skills flourish. They still primarily imitate others when they play, but they also start to interact more with others and even delve into some pretend play, too. Here are some specific skills they start exhibiting at this stage.

Gross Motor Skills

- Walks and runs
- Coordinates their movements for play
- Jumps with their feet together
- Walks up and down stairs
- Throws a ball into a box
- Uses ride-on toys

Fine Motor Skills

- Uses fingers and thumbs to hold crayons
- Opens containers
- Turns the pages of a book
- Scribble-writes with writing tools
- Builds with four or more blocks
- Turns over and pours out containers

Language and Social-Emotional Skills

- Starts to use two-word phrases
- Can name objects in pictures
- Understands action words
- Starts to use pronouns (you, my, me)
- Can identify three to five body parts
- Follows simple two-step directions
- Interacts with others during play
- May play with toys without mouthing them
- Enjoys directing play

24 to 36 Months

After toddlers turn two years old, their cognitive, language, and social-emotional learning take the lead over the previous focus on physical development. Social-emotional growth means a toddler also has the desire for more independence. Combine that with a toddler's expanding language skills, which help them communicate their needs and wants, and this can prove to be a challenging time for caregivers! Here are some important skills toddlers are typically developing at this stage.

Gross Motor Skills

- Kicks a ball forward
- Can stand on tiptoes
- Pulls toys behind them while walking
- Carries large toys while walking
- Can ride a tricycle
- Catches a large ball
- Jumps over an object
- Walks along a balance beam

Fine Motor Skills

- Picks up small objects using their fingers in a pincer grasp
- Turns door handles
- Screws a lid on a container
- Can string large beads
- Starts to draw squares and circles

Language and Social-Emotional Skills

- Uses two- to four-word sentences
- Is understood when they talk
- Demonstrates increasing independence
- Plays make-believe
- Begins to sort objects by colors and shapes
- Starts to understand "same" and "different"
- Enjoys listening to and telling stories
- Starts to count and understand numbers
- Becomes increasingly inventive during play

Each activity in this book includes easy-to-understand icons indicating the developmental skills and learning concepts that activity reinforces. If you're looking to work on certain skills with your toddler, you can use the icons to help you choose specific activities geared toward those skills. However, always feel free to follow your toddler's curiosity and interests first and foremost. And, remember, play has such intrinsic educational and developmental benefits, many of the activities will actually strengthen more skills than those represented by the icons. No matter what activity you choose, you can be sure your toddler will be learning and developing important skills every step of the way!

Skills Learned

COLORS

LISTENING

SENSORY DEVELOPMENT

CREATIVITY

MINDFULNESS

SHAPES AND LETTERS

EARLY LITERACY

NUMBERS AND COUNTING

SOCIAL-EMOTIONAL DEVELOPMENT

FINE MOTOR SKILLS

ORAL MOTOR DEVELOPMENT

SORTING

GROSS MOTOR SKILLS

PATTERNS

VISUAL SPATIAL SKILLS

IMAGINATION

PROBLEM-SOLVING

LANGUAGE DEVELOPMENT

SCIENCE

Safety First!

I've tried to make each activity as safe as possible for you and your little one. Some activities include a specific note of *Caution!* In addition, here are some general safety guidelines that you should follow while doing every activity in this book.

- Consider your toddler's development level and abilities when choosing activities. Monitor and assist your toddler as needed, especially when doing advanced activities.

- Avoid activities that call for small materials if your toddler mouths objects during play.

- *Always* supervise your toddler closely during any water play and *never* leave bins, containers, or bathtubs of water unattended.

- Keep your toddler away from sharp scissors and other potentially hazardous tools. If possible, perform any prep requiring these tools when your toddler is not present.

- Whenever possible, choose nontoxic, kid-friendly art supplies and materials. If a material is new to you and likely to come in contact with your toddler's skin, test it on a small area of your skin and your toddler's skin before play.

- Some play materials and setups could pose tripping, slipping, falling, choking, and strangulation hazards if left unsupervised. Take down and put away all play setups and materials after play has ended.

- All of the activities are designed for your toddler *and you*. Always supervise during play.

How to Use this Book

Each chapter ahead includes about 20 activities that are based on a specific toddler-friendly theme: active play, exploration and experimentation, creative activities, imaginative play, and outdoor fun. Pick and choose the themes that work for you at any given time, and feel free to jump around!

My aim for this book, even more so than for my previous toddler activity books, is to make it super easy for you to incorporate tons of intentional play, build meaningful connections, experience playful learning, and enjoy some plain old fun with your toddler. I hope these activities will quickly prove that toddler fun doesn't require a complicated setup or a long list of materials.

Follow these tips to keep the fun and learning high and the complexity low.

Prep when possible. With the intention of quick-and-easy fun, most activities in this book require no prep at all. However, up to five minutes of prep was included for some of the activities when necessary for the safety of your toddler or the success of the activity. Use your discretion (and the safety guidelines on page 10) to decide whether to include your toddler in prep.

Check the messiness scale. There is a time and place for toddler mess-making. In fact, there's an entire chapter of messy activities in my book The Outdoor Toddler Activity Book. However, when you have limited time, a small space, or are just feeling overwhelmed, a mess is not what you need. Most of the activities in this book are no-mess or low-mess. Each activity includes a messiness scale to indicate its mess factor and help you decide which activities are right for you. A one on the scale means the activity has very few messy materials. A five on the scale indicates very messy materials; your toddler will likely end up muddy, wet, covered in paint, and/or dirty! If you are up for some messy play, I recommend you first lay some old towels or a disposable tablecloth on the play area to make cleanup time easier. Or, better yet, if possible, do the messy activities outside!

Consider your time—and your toddler's attention span. Each activity in this book can be completed in under 20 minutes (including prep time), and therefore is well suited to a busy parent's schedule and a toddler's short attention span. However, we all know a toddler's attention span shifts from day to day, and sometimes from minute to minute! Use the time estimates that accompany each activity to help choose the right activity to fit your toddler's attention span and temperament at the moment.

Use what you have around the house. Unusual materials, tricky tools, and complex prep just don't mix with toddlerhood. No toddler parent or caregiver has time or patience for them, anyway. That's why I've designed the activities in this book to use as few materials as possible, almost all of which are everyday items. Some activities use basic kids' craft supplies, like construction paper or washable markers. However, most utilize typical household items, like a muffin pan, plastic food storage containers, or the laundry basket. There are even a few activities that require no materials at all!

Use the tips to adjust. Each activity includes a handy tip to help you modify the activity to your toddler's or your specific needs. These types of tips include:

- **Simple Swap.** This tip includes substitutions for one or more of an activity's materials.
- **Age Adaptation.** This tip includes ideas for adjusting the activity for an older or a younger child.
- **Next Level.** This tip includes ways to add to the learning and/or creativity of an activity.

Let the activities inspire you! The material lists, prep instructions, and activity steps are provided to make activities *easier* for you, not to limit you. If you need to replace materials on the list with ones you have on hand, go for it. Follow your own or your toddler's whim and try a different way of doing an activity. Go ahead and use numbers instead of the alphabet. Let these activities be a jumping-off point for you and your toddler and see where they can take you!

Always follow your toddler's lead. Never force an activity on a toddler who may be resistant for whatever reason. Every activity naturally integrates developmental skills and early learning concepts that include color identification, numbers and counting, the ABCs, and more. So, whatever they choose, they can't lose!

Every little bit counts! This book was written to offer you and your toddler ideas for meaningful, easy play whenever you choose to use it. I would be shocked if a toddler parent or caregiver actually read this entire book straight through or attempted to do every single activity with their toddler. Every little bit of intentional play and connection with your toddler adds up to make a *huge* difference in your toddler's learning and development. It's perfectly okay to skim through it while your toddler is napping in search of an activity from chapter 2 for later on in the day. Or keep the book by your bedside and thumb through it to find a creative activity from chapter 4 for your toddler's next playdate. There's lots of easy fun and learning right at your fingertips!

* 2 *
Wiggle, Jump & Play!

Anyone who cares for a toddler knows about "the wiggles": those bursts of energy when a little one simply has to be moving, jumping, touching, wriggling, and . . . wiggling! It can be exhausting to watch—let alone to try to keep up with—but all of that movement helps with a toddler's brain development. Did you know, for example, that when a toddler is running, they are not only developing motor skills, but also learning body awareness and balance?

So I'm inviting you to embrace your little one's wiggles and use the fun and easy active play ideas in this chapter to keep your toddler's busy body happy and their brain learning. Who knows? You may even be able to tire them out long enough for naptime!

Color Surprise Match

COLORS

GROSS MOTOR
SKILLS

VISUAL SPATIAL
SKILLS

Make color learning super fun for your little one by combining the element of surprise with an action-packed indoor color hunt!

Messiness: 2
Prep Time: Less than
5 minutes
Activity Time: 15 minutes

MATERIALS

Scissors

3 index cards or
3 index-card-size
rectangles of white
paper

Washable markers in
red, orange, yellow,
green, blue, and purple

Empty tissue box

PREP

Cut the index cards or rectangles of paper in half.

STEPS

1. Have your toddler scribble on each card with a different-color marker. Review each color with him while he is scribbling with that color marker. Have him place each color card in the empty tissue box.

2. Invite your toddler to shake the box (and himself, of course!), and then have him reach inside and pull out a color card. Ask him what color it is.

3. Have him look around the house to find something that matches the color.

4. Tell him to call out "[Color] match!" when he finds it.

5. Have your toddler go back to the box of color cards and choose another one. Repeat until the box is empty.

SIMPLE SWAP: Paint sample cards, found in any store that sells home paint, can also be used as instant color cards.

CAUTION! Be sure to keep your toddler away from sharp scissors.

Puppy Nose Soccer

Do you have balloons hanging around after a party? Grab a laundry basket and play an imaginative puppy-themed game of soccer!

Messiness: **1**
Prep Time: **5 minutes**
Activity Time: **15 minutes**

MATERIALS

3 to 5 balloons

Laundry basket

GROSS MOTOR
SKILLS

IMAGINATION

SENSORY
DEVELOPMENT

PREP

1. Blow up the balloons and scatter them on the floor of the room.

2. Place the laundry basket on its side in a part of the room far away from most of the balloons.

STEPS

1. Discuss the characteristics of dogs with your toddler, such as how dogs stand on four legs, have an incredible sense of smell, bark, and wag their tails when they're happy. Practice pretending to be puppies.

2. Tell your toddler it's time to use her puppy nose to first find and then push and roll each balloon into the laundry basket. Say "Good puppy!" and pat your toddler on the head each time she gets a balloon in the "goal."

NEXT LEVEL: Use a permanent marker to write a different number (starting with 1) on each balloon. Then, have your toddler find and roll the balloons into the goal in numerical order. Or, if you have more than one child playing, have them race to see who can roll their balloon into the goal first.

CAUTION! Be sure to never leave balloons unsupervised, as they can pose a choking hazard.

GROSS MOTOR
SKILLS

IMAGINATION

SCIENCE

SENSORY
DEVELOPMENT

Birds of a Feather Tag

A little imagination helps the standard game of tag take flight!
This game is a great way to get your toddler moving while they
learn some bird basics.

Messiness: **3**
Prep Time: **5 minutes**
Activity Time: **15 minutes**

MATERIALS

Masking tape

Craft feathers in
various colors

Medium-size plastic
bins, one per color of
feather

PREP

1. Make loops of masking tape, sticky-side out, and
   place one (or more) around each player's shirt
   sleeve. (Make sure all long hair is pulled up so it
   can't get stuck in the tape.)

2. Put the feathers in the bins, making sure to have
   only one color of feather in each one. Place the
   bins in various locations around the room
   (or yard).

STEPS

1. Explain that birds have feathers that help them
   fly. Tell the toddlers to pretend that they are
   now all birds, but they need their feathers!
   Show them how to flap their "wings" by having
   them bring their hands toward their chests and
   moving their elbows up and down.

2. Explain the rules of the game:
   - Tell the toddlers that they are going to help
     each other get their feathers so they can
     pretend to fly.
   - Then, on the count of three, the toddlers
     must run around the room (or yard), grab
     feathers from the bins, and try to stick the
     feathers onto each others' sticky tape.
   - When a player's tape is entirely covered in
     feathers, they can now pretend to fly like a
     bird! That player must now stop picking up
     feathers. Instead they must flap their wings,
     pretend to fly around, and caw like a bird.

3. Count to three and watch them go! Play continues until all players have become birds— you may have to fully feather the last player yourself so they can take flight, too!

AGE ADAPTATION: Add some color learning and make the game more challenging for older kids by assigning each player a color. Simply stick a different-color feather on each player's tape to indicate their color. Then, make a rule that only matching-color feathers can be stuck on each player. For this adaptation, mix up the feathers so that each bin has different-colored feathers in it.

COLORS

**GROSS MOTOR
SKILLS**

**SENSORY
DEVELOPMENT**

Colorful Sensory Crawl

Turn old gift wrapping ribbon, crepe paper streamers, yarn, or lightweight scarves into a color-filled sensory activity to captivate your toddler!

Messiness: **3**
Prep Time: **5 minutes**
Activity Time: **10 minutes**

MATERIALS

Scissors

Various string-like materials, such as ribbon, yarn, and crepe paper streamers, in various colors

Painter's tape

Coffee table or dining table

PREP

1. Cut multiple lengths of the materials.

2. Tape the materials onto the edges of the table so they hang down near the floor. Use different-color materials on each side of the table, if possible.

STEPS

1. Encourage your toddler to crawl back and forth under the table, through the hanging materials.

2. Encourage your toddler to feel all the different materials and talk about how they look and feel using words like *soft, shiny, stretchy,* and *scratchy.* Ask your child to identify the colors of each material, too.

NEXT LEVEL: If you have some bells or other objects that jingle, tie them onto some of the materials to add an element of sound to the activity.

CAUTION! Be sure to keep your toddler away from sharp scissors. Supervise your toddler during play, and take down the activity as soon as you and your toddler have finished playing, as the materials used can be a choking and strangulation hazard.

Indoor Shape Skating

Take your toddler ice-skating—right in the house! Tissue-box ice skates and tape shapes make it fun and educational, too.

GROSS MOTOR SKILLS

IMAGINATION

SHAPES AND LETTERS

Messiness: **2**
Prep Time: **5 minutes**
Activity Time: **10 minutes**

MATERIALS

Painter's tape

Scissors

2 empty rectangular tissue boxes

Wax paper

PREP

1. Use tape and scissors, as needed, to wrap the bottom half of each tissue box in wax paper. If one side of the wax paper is waxier than the other, make sure that the waxier side is facing out.

2. Use painter's tape to create giant shapes (circle, square, rectangle, and triangle) on the floor.

STEPS

1. Help your toddler put the boxes on his feet, like ice skates.

2. Ask him to identify one of the tape shapes on the floor. Encourage him to shuffle his feet to skate along the tape lines of the shape. Be nearby and ready to help keep your toddler upright and safe!

3. Repeat with each tape shape.

AGE ADAPTATION: Add more challenging shape learning by calling out shapes for your child to find and skate to.

CAUTION! Be sure to keep your toddler away from sharp scissors. Supervise your toddler during play, and never leave the activity set up and unsupervised, as the materials used can be a fall or injury hazard.

**GROSS MOTOR
SKILLS**

**SENSORY
DEVELOPMENT**

**VISUAL SPATIAL
SKILLS**

Transportation Hide-and-Seek

My son Sawyer would spend hours as a toddler driving his toy trucks and tractors around the house. All that crawling is great for motor skill development and sensory regulation, so let's make it even more fun with a transportation-themed hide-and-seek game!

Messiness: **2**
Prep Time: **None**
Activity Time: **15 minutes**

MATERIALS

Various transportation toys, such as cars, trucks, and trains

Medium-size plastic bin

STEPS

1. Together with your toddler, gather all of the transportation toys you can find in your home. Place them in the plastic bin.

2. Have your toddler cover her eyes while you hide the cars, trucks, and trains randomly around the house. Place the empty bin on its side.

3. Have your toddler hunt for the transportation toys and drive each one back to the bin, crawling on her hands and knees. Encourage your toddler to make lots of beeping, honking, and other transportation-toy sounds!

NEXT LEVEL: Use a marker and blank label stickers to label each transportation toy with a number (1 through 5 or 1 through 10). Place a cardboard box on its side. Draw numbered parking spots corresponding with the numbers on the toys inside the box for the transportation toys to park.

CAUTION! Make sure to choose transportation toys suitable and safe for your toddler's age.

Count and Fly Balloon

Is there anything more exciting for a toddler than watching a balloon fly and twirl through the air as it deflates? Harness that excitement to inspire some fun counting practice and lots of movement with your little one.

Messiness: **1**
Prep Time: **None**
Activity Time: **10 minutes**

MATERIALS

1 balloon, uninflated

GROSS MOTOR SKILLS

123

NUMBERS AND COUNTING

STEPS

1. Practice counting to five with your toddler.

2. Have him count to five while you blow a big breath into the balloon with each number. When he says the number five, hold the balloon up in the air and let it go so it flies wildly around the room while deflating.

3. Share in your child's excitement, then have him run to find the balloon and bring it back for another round of count and fly. Repeat for lots of counting and wild balloon chasing.

AGE ADAPTATION: For an older toddler, try counting to a higher number. Or, if he is able, allow him to blow up the balloon while you count.

CAUTION! Supervise your toddler during play, and never leave the activity materials unsupervised, as they can be a choking and injury hazard.

Color Block Sweep and Sort

Your toddler's own colorful building blocks make a great tool for some active color-sorting fun.

COLORS

GROSS MOTOR
SKILLS

123

NUMBERS AND
COUNTING

SORTING

Messiness: **3**
Prep Time: **5 minutes**
Activity Time: **15 minutes**

MATERIALS

Kids' or full-size broom

Tape

Construction paper,
one sheet per
block color

Interlocking building
blocks in various colors

PREP

1. Tape different-colored sheets of construction paper onto the floor along one end of the room.

2. Scatter building blocks that are the same colors as the construction paper randomly on the floor at the other end of the room.

STEPS

1. Review the colors of the papers on the floor with your toddler.

2. Have your toddler use a broom to sweep the blocks from the other side of the room onto their matching-color papers.

AGE ADAPTATION: For an older toddler, add number learning by placing a random number magnet on each paper for your toddler to sweep the corresponding number of matching-color blocks onto that paper.

NEXT LEVEL: Does your little one have any construction machine toys? Have your child use a bulldozer toy or dump truck toy to push or haul the blocks to their matching-color papers.

Teddy Bear Taxi

Encourage indoor active play, as well as beneficial language and social skills, with an imaginative taxi-themed activity!

Messiness: 1
Prep Time: **Less than 5 minutes**
Activity Time: **15 minutes**

MATERIALS

Indoor toddler ride-on toy

Teddy bears or other stuffed animals

Medium-size plastic bin (optional)

Duct tape (optional)

PREP

If your child's ride-on toy doesn't have room for a teddy bear to ride along with her, add a riding basket to it by duct-taping a plastic bin onto the front or back of the toy.

STEPS

1. Hold the teddy bear and ask your toddler get on the ride-on toy. Tell her she is now a taxi driver.

2. Have her drive around the room.

3. Wave one of the teddy bear's arms and call out, *"Taxi! Taxi!"* to get your little taxi driver to stop. Have the teddy bear ask for a ride to a different room. Use clever street names for the rooms, such as Bedroom Boulevard, Kitchen Street, or Playroom Way.

4. Place the teddy bear on the ride-on toy (or in the attached bin) and send the taxi on its way.

5. Have your toddler come back for another passenger! Each time, have the passenger direct your child to a different room. Encourage lots of **polite conversation and good manners between the taxi driver and her passengers.**

SIMPLE SWAP: No ride-on toy? No problem! Play this taxi game using a toy car or truck and toy figures small enough to fit inside it.

CAUTION! Make sure to choose toys that are suitable and safe for your toddler.

GROSS MOTOR SKILLS

IMAGINATION

LANGUAGE DEVELOPMENT

SOCIAL-EMOTIONAL DEVELOPMENT

**FINE MOTOR
SKILLS**

**LANGUAGE
DEVELOPMENT**

PROBLEM-SOLVING

**VISUAL SPATIAL
SKILLS**

Under Roll

Here's a fun way for your little one to use everyday household objects to practice hand-eye coordination while learning about size comparison and the concept of under.

Messiness: **1**
Prep Time: **None**
Activity Time: **10 minutes**

MATERIALS

Various household furniture a ball could roll under, such as a coffee table, dining table, dining chairs, and kids' table and chairs

Kids' toy balls in a variety of sizes

STEPS

1. Position yourself on the opposite side of one of the pieces of furniture from your toddler. Roll one of the balls under the furniture to your child.

2. Have him try rolling the ball back to you under the furniture. Each time someone rolls a ball, be sure to say the word *under*.

3. Experiment with rolling balls of different sizes under different pieces of furniture. Compare and contrast the sizes of the balls using words such as *small, medium, large, smaller, larger, smallest,* **and** *largest*.

NEXT LEVEL: If you have a little time and some cardboard boxes, turn the boxes upside down and cut arches out of opposite sides. Add number learning to the activity by writing a different number on the side of each box (starting at 1). Position the boxes randomly throughout the room, then call out numbers for your toddler to find and roll balls through those boxes.

CAUTION! Supervise your toddler during play, and never leave the activity set up and unsupervised, as the materials used can be an injury hazard.

Color Dot Simon Says

Add some color learning and lots of fun to the classic favorite Simon Says. All you need is sidewalk chalk!

Messiness: **3**
Prep Time: **5 minutes**
Activity Time: **15 minutes**

MATERIALS

Sidewalk chalk in a variety of colors

Sidewalk

COLORS

GROSS MOTOR SKILLS

LISTENING

PREP

Review the names of the colors with your child while you use the sidewalk chalk to draw large dots of different colors along the sidewalk. You can ask her to help color in the circles, if desired.

STEPS

1. Play Simon Says using the different-colored dots and various actions.

2. Make sure your toddler knows to only perform an action when you say, "Simon says . . ."

3. To test your toddler, don't say "Simon says . . ." every once in a while and see what they do—or don't do! Here are some commands to try:

    a. Simon says "jump on red."
    b. Simon says "sit on green."
    c. Simon says "dance on yellow."
    d. Simon says "march on blue."

SIMPLE SWAP: Playing indoors? Tape different-colored sheets of construction paper on the floor to use instead of chalk dots.

CAUTION! Supervise your toddler during play and never leave the materials unsupervised, as the materials used can be a choking hazard.

TP Toss and Count

GROSS MOTOR SKILLS

123 NUMBERS AND COUNTING

VISUAL SPATIAL SKILLS

Use your stockpile of toilet paper rolls for a silly potty-themed tossing game. Your toddler can practice motor skills and get excited for potty training at the same time!

Messiness: **1**
Prep Time: **Less than 5 minutes**
Activity Time: **10 minutes**

MATERIALS

6 or more rolls of toilet paper or plastic ball pit balls

2 laundry baskets

PREP

1. Have your toddler help gather and place 5 or 10 rolls of toilet paper in a laundry basket.

2. Keep that basket nearby and position another basket about a foot away.

STEPS

1. Talk to him about how big kids go to the bathroom on the potty, wipe with toilet paper, and then flush the toilet. Explain that you're going to play a potty game now to help get them ready!

2. Explain the rules of the game to your toddler.

   - Standing 1 foot from the basket, toss a roll of toilet paper into it and count, *"One flush!"*
   - Take a step back from the basket, and repeat, throwing another roll of toilet paper into the basket and counting, *"Two flushes."*
   - Continue tossing and counting.
   - If you miss the basket, you must return to the starting position 1 foot away from the basket and start over from the beginning.

3. Invite your toddler to play the game, tossing and counting. Celebrate every time they count flushes to encourage excitement in going on the potty.

AGE ADAPTATION: Allow younger toddlers to stay in one spot while tossing instead of stepping back each time.

Animal Hide-and-Find

Use your toddler's stuffed animals or animal toys to inspire imaginative animal movements during a simple game of hide-and-find. The addition of a toy wagon adds pulling movements that are beneficial for sensory development, too.

Messiness: **1**
Prep Time: **None**
Activity Time: **10 minutes**

MATERIALS

Various stuffed animals or other animal toys

Toy wagon

STEPS

1. Gather up a bunch of stuffed animals or animal toys. Help your toddler identify each animal and imitate their movements. For example, a snake slithers along the floor, a monkey swings its arms around, a horse gallops, and a dog runs.

2. Have your toddler cover his eyes while you hide the stuffed animals around the house.

3. Invite your toddler to take the wagon and go searching for animals. When he finds one, have him imitate that animal's movements, and then put the stuffed animal in his wagon.

4. Repeat until all the stuffed animals have been found and are in the wagon.

SIMPLE SWAP: Don't have an indoor toy wagon? Hook a belt through the side of a laundry basket for your toddler to pull and use as a wagon.

CAUTION! Supervise your toddler during play and never leave the materials unsupervised, as the materials used can be an injury hazard.

GROSS MOTOR SKILLS

IMAGINATION

ORAL MOTOR DEVELOPMENT

SCIENCE

SENSORY DEVELOPMENT

GROSS MOTOR
SKILLS

SENSORY
DEVELOPMENT

SHAPES AND
LETTERS

VISUAL SPATIAL
SKILLS

ABC Tightrope Walker

Inspire your toddler to practice essential balancing skills with this imaginative tightrope game. A creative addition encourages alphabet learning, too.

Messiness: **2**
Prep Time: **5 minutes**
Activity Time: **10 minutes**

MATERIALS

Painter's tape

Letter flashcards

PREP

1. Use painter's tape to make a long line on the floor that goes from one area of the house to another.

2. Tape the letter flashcards onto the line on the floor so they are evenly spaced and in alphabetical order.

STEPS

1. Tell your toddler you've created an alphabet tightrope, and that she should pretend it is actually high up in the air. Ask her if she is daring enough to walk along it!

2. Invite her to walk across the tightrope carefully, keeping her balance. When she comes to a flashcard, help her identify and say the letter.

3. Keep going until she has walked to each flashcard and said all the letters.

SIMPLE SWAP: Use number, shape, or animal flashcards to change up the learning. No flashcards? Make some by writing letters, numbers, or shapes on sticky notes.

Alphabet Balloon Ball

Combine gross motor movement, hand-eye coordination practice, and alphabet learning using a simple balloon and some flyswatters!

Messiness: **1**
Prep Time: **5 minutes**
Activity Time: **10 minutes**

MATERIALS

String

Painter's tape

Balloon, inflated

2 flyswatters

PREP

Use string and tape to hang the balloon from the ceiling or an interior door frame. Make sure your toddler will be able to reach the balloon with a flyswatter.

STEPS

1. Grab a flyswatter and give your toddler the other one. Stand on each side of the balloon. Use the flyswatter to hit the balloon toward your child and say "A!"

2. Have him use his flyswatter to hit the balloon back toward you and say "B!"

3. Repeat, hitting the balloon back and forth while saying each letter of the alphabet. See if you can get through the entire alphabet!

AGE ADAPTATION: With an older toddler, try swatting a loose balloon back and forth instead of hanging it from the ceiling. Still say the alphabet while swatting it.

CAUTION! Supervise your toddler during play and never leave the materials unsupervised, as they can be a choking and strangulation hazard.

GROSS MOTOR SKILLS

SENSORY DEVELOPMENT

SHAPES AND LETTERS

VISUAL SPATIAL SKILLS

GROSS MOTOR
SKILLS

LANGUAGE
DEVELOPMENT

SENSORY
DEVELOPMENT

VISUAL SPATIAL
SKILLS

Arrow Obstacle Course

Obstacle courses are a great way to get kids moving indoors. Add some arrows to the obstacles for added language and spatial learning.

Messiness: **3**
Prep Time: **5 minutes**
Activity Time: **15 minutes**

MATERIALS

Various household items, such as couch cushions, pillows, laundry baskets, dining chairs, and a coffee table

Marker

Paper plates or construction paper

Painter's tape

PREP

1. Make a simple obstacle course by placing various household objects every few feet down a hallway or across a room.

2. Draw a large arrow on each plate and tape the plates onto each obstacle to indicate whether your child should go up (over it), down (under it), left, or right (around it). Here are some ideas to try:

   - Stack two couch cushions and label them with an arrow pointing up so she climbs over them.
   - Place a pillow on the floor and label it with an arrow pointing left so she goes around it to the left. Then, place another pillow on the floor and label with an arrow pointing right so she goes around it to the right. And so on.
   - Position a dining chair and label it with an arrow pointing down so she crawls under it.
   - Position an upside-down laundry basket and label it with an arrow pointing up so she climbs over it.

STEPS

1. Invite your toddler to walk through the obstacle course with you. Review the arrows and directional words *up, over, down, under, left, right,* and *around*.

2. Allow your toddler to go through the obstacle course. Prompt her with directional words as she comes to new obstacles.

NEXT LEVEL: Try using a timer (such as one on your smartphone) to time your toddler as she goes through the obstacle course. Then challenge her to try again and beat her time.

CAUTION! Supervise your toddler during play and never leave the activity set up and unsupervised, as the materials used can be an injury hazard.

GROSS MOTOR SKILLS

123

NUMBERS AND COUNTING

SENSORY DEVELOPMENT

SHAPES AND LETTERS

Sidewalk Shape Hop

Sidewalk chalk makes outdoor learning super easy—and fun, too! Simply draw some shapes, numbers, and winding lines for a sidewalk path that will have your little one hopping and counting.

Messiness: **1**
Prep Time: **5 minutes**
Activity Time: **10 minutes**

MATERIALS

Sidewalk chalk

Sidewalk

PREP

1. Use sidewalk chalk to draw random basic shapes (circles, squares, rectangles, triangles, diamonds, ovals), each containing a different number (from 1 through 10), six feet or so apart on the sidewalk.

2. Connect the shapes with winding lines to create a long path of number shapes.

STEPS

1. Invite your toddler to walk along the number-shape path, trying to stay within the winding lines.

2. When he gets to a shape, help him identify it and the number inside it. Then have him hop on the shape as many as times as the number.

3. Keep going until all the shapes and numbers have been identified—and hopped on!

SIMPLE SWAP: Can't get outside? Use painter's tape and paper plates (taped down) to make a similar path right on the floor indoors. Simply use a marker to draw a large shape and number on each plate.

Musical Matching Game

This educational spin on musical chairs can be played with multiple toddlers, siblings of various ages, or with just one toddler. Plus, it can be customized to whatever learning concepts you'd like.

Messiness: **1**
Prep Time: **5 minutes**
Activity Time: **15 minutes**

MATERIALS

Marker

Index cards or squares of white paper

Music

PREP

1. Use the marker and index cards to make two sets of number cards, numbered 1 through 10.

2. Place one set in a circle on the floor in the middle of the room. Then, place the other set in a row on the floor along the side of the room. Place both sets of cards faceup so you and your toddler can see the numbers.

STEPS

1. Have your toddler dance around the circle of number cards while you play music.

2. Randomly stop the music and have her pick up the number card she stopped at, identify the number, run to the row of number cards, and place it on its matching number card.

3. Then, have her return to the circle of number cards and begin dancing around it again when you restart the music.

4. Repeat, randomly stopping the music for your toddler to stop, grab a number card, and find its match, until all number cards have been matched.

AGE ADAPTATION: Try this game with any learning concepts your little one is working on, such as basic shapes, letters of the alphabet, or colors. For more advanced learning, create one set of cards with numbers and the other set with corresponding numbers of dots.

Rainbow Order Relay

COLORS

GROSS MOTOR
SKILLS

VISUAL SPATIAL
SKILLS

Add some colorful fun to an active relay game that can be played inside or out!

Messiness: **1**
Prep Time: **None**
Activity Time: **20 minutes**

MATERIALS

Construction paper, one sheet per each color of the rainbow

Tape

STEPS

1. Together with your child, use the paper to review the colors of the rainbow. Then, have him cover his eyes while you hide each sheet of paper in a different spot in the house.

2. Call out the first color of the rainbow, *"Red!"*, and have your toddler run around the house looking for the red paper. Once he finds it, have him bring it to you and tape it onto the floor.

3. Then call out the next color of the rainbow, *"Orange!"* Have him run and find that piece of paper, bring it back, and tape it next to the red paper on the floor.

4. Repeat for each remaining color of the rainbow (*"Yellow!"*, *"Green!"*, *"Blue!"*, and *"Purple!"*) until all the sheets of paper have been found and are taped down in rainbow order.

5. Invite your toddler to hop along the paper rainbow, starting with red. Encourage him to call out the colors as he hops on them.

NEXT LEVEL: Tape the sheets of paper down onto the floor and ask your toddler to go on a color hunt around the house for objects that are the same colors. Have him arrange the objects on their matching-color papers.

Follow the Marching-Band Leader

Take imaginative marching band play to the next level with this follow-the-leader listening game.

Messiness: **None**
Prep Time: **None**
Activity Time: **10 minutes**

MATERIALS

Nothing!

GROSS MOTOR SKILLS

IMAGINATION

LISTENING

ORAL MOTOR DEVELOPMENT

STEPS

1. Have a talk with your toddler about marching bands and the instruments played by members of the band.

2. Together, pretend to be band members: march around the house and "play" the various instruments, being sure to make the sounds of each instrument!

3. Let your toddler have a turn being the band-leader while you follow her and copy her movements and sounds.

AGE ADAPTATION: Try clapping out different beats for an older child to mimic and clap back.

10

Ways to Play with Your Toddler During Car Travel

1. **Dashboard Tap:** Tap out a beat on the dashboard for your toddler to clap back.

2. **Window Binoculars:** Offer your toddler toy binoculars to use while looking out the window and ask her to tell you what she sees.

3. **Baking Pan Magnet Play:** Offer your toddler magnets to play with on a metal baking sheet pan.

4. **Window Cling Fun:** Offer window cling decorations for arranging and playing with on the window.

5. **Count the Cows:** Count cows or other animals or objects you see out the window.

6. **Seated Freeze Dance:** Play music and invite your child to dance in his seat, using his upper body. Tell your child that when you turn the music off he has to freeze in place. Turn the music off and on several times. Giggling is allowed during a freeze!

7. **Road Sign Alphabet:** Look for letters of the alphabet on road signs.

8. **Puppet Show:** Give your toddler hand puppets or finger puppets to act out a puppet show.

9. **Spy the Rainbow:** Look for each color, in rainbow order, out the window.

10. **Simple Sensory Bottle:** Make a sensory bottle by filling a clear plastic water bottle with dry rice and different-color buttons. Invite your toddler to shake it each time she spots an object you asked her to look for.

* 3 *
Explore Your World

A toddler's natural curiosity and inclination to play drive early learning and development. They are endlessly absorbing new sights and sounds around them during play. They store all of that new information away to call on later. That means the more unique hands-on experiences we give our toddlers, the better.

From squishy sensory materials to toddler-friendly science experiments to simple games you can play on the go, the activities in this chapter will have you and your toddler seeing and experiencing the world all around you in fun and interesting ways. Use the hands-on ideas ahead to harness your toddler's natural curiosity and channel it into fun and learning—and away from toddler mischief.

Simple Sink Science—3 Ways!

COLORS

PROBLEM-SOLVING

SCIENCE

SENSORY
DEVELOPMENT

When my kids were toddlers, they loved working beside me at the kitchen sink. A bit of soapy water, some plastic bins, and a sponge was all they needed. The sink can also be a great place for some toddler science fun: it lets your little one experiment and play while containing the mess and ensuring easy cleanup!

Messiness: **1**
Prep Time: **None**
Activity Time: **20 minutes**

MATERIALS

Candy Color Magic

Sink and stepstool

Shallow plastic bin

Colorful candies

Water

Easy Ice Melt

Sink and stepstool

Ice cubes

Various plastic food storage containers

Water

Measuring cups

Salt shaker

Color Surprise Volcano

Sink and stepstool

Various plastic food storage containers

Baking soda

Food coloring in various colors

Squeeze bottle filled with vinegar

CANDY COLOR MAGIC

1. Have your toddler help line the edges of the inside of a shallow plastic bin with different-colored candies.

2. Carefully add some warm water to the bin, just until it touches the candies. Watch as the colors begin to dissolve and mix in the water.

EASY ICE MELT

1. Place some ice cubes inside the sink. Fill various small containers with different temperature (but kid-friendly) water and place them in the sink.

2. Offer some measuring cups for scooping the water from the containers and pouring onto the ice. Offer a salt shaker for experimenting with how salt affects the ice.

COLOR SURPRISE VOLCANO

1. Fill an inch or so of a small container with baking soda. Add a few drops of food coloring, then cover it with a bit more baking soda.

2. Place the container in the bottom of the sink. Repeat with other containers, using different colors of food coloring. Give your toddler a squeeze bottle filled with vinegar to squirt into each container and watch the colorful "volcanoes" erupt!

SIMPLE SWAP: If a sink and stepstool won't work for you, try these experiments outside on a sunny day or in a large shallow plastic bin on some towels on the floor.

CAUTION! Supervise your toddler during play and never leave the activity set up and unsupervised, as the materials can be an injury hazard. Always stay near your toddler while they are on the stepstool to assist them and prevent falls.

FINE MOTOR
SKILLS

MINDFULNESS

SENSORY
DEVELOPMENT

Two-Ingredient Instant Dough

Playdough is always a toddler favorite, and for good reason! Squishing and squeezing the "dough" is not only fun, it strengthens their fine motor skills and provides calming sensory input. Here's a quick-and-easy recipe to make some dough with your toddler.

Messiness: **4**
Prep Time: **None**
Activity Time: **20 minutes**

MATERIALS

Measuring cups

1 cup kid-friendly scented hair conditioner

2 cups cornstarch, plus more as needed

Mixing bowl

Wooden spoon

STEPS

1. Together with your toddler, add the conditioner and cornstarch to the mixing bowl.

2. Stir thoroughly until it starts to form a dough and begins to pull away from the sides of the bowl.

3. Knead the dough with your hands until it reaches the desired consistency. Add more cornstarch, as needed.

4. Offer the scented dough to your child. Ask your child to describe the scent and feel of the dough, as well as how it makes your child feel to play with it.

NEXT LEVEL: Add to the fun and learning by making impressions in the dough with washable objects and toys, such as a shaped cookie cutter, a potato masher, buttons, a toy car, a plastic clothespin, or a small plastic animal toy.

CAUTION! Supervise your toddler during play and never leave the activity set up and unsupervised, as the materials can be an injury hazard. This dough is not taste-safe and not suitable for children who put objects in their mouths during play.

Colander Cereal Color Match

COLORS

FINE MOTOR SKILLS

If you and your toddler have never tried this popular colander and pipe cleaner activity, you are both in for a treat! It's simple yet so enthralling for little ones, and this version adds some color matching and threading to your toddler's colander play.

Messiness: **3**
Prep Time: **None**
Activity Time: **15 minutes**

MATERIALS

Plastic or metal colander

Pipe cleaners in colors that match the cereal

Colorful O-shaped cereal, placed in a container

STEPS

1. Position the colander upside down and have your toddler thread at least one of each color of pipe cleaner through the colander's holes.

2. Provide a container of colorful O-shaped cereal and show your toddler how to choose one O, identify its color, and then thread it onto a matching-color pipe cleaner sticking out of the colander.

3. Have him repeat choosing, matching, and threading Os on his own until all of them have been threaded, or as his interest allows.

AGE ADAPTATION: Skip the color matching if your toddler is too young or if you only have plain O-shaped cereal. It will still be fun as a creative sculpture and fine motor activity.

CAUTION! Monitor your toddler closely when playing with small objects.

FINE MOTOR
SKILLS

PROBLEM-SOLVING

SCIENCE

SORTING

Magnet Move and Sort

Magnets have always been fascinating to my little ones. Try this activity to get your toddler playing and experimenting with magnetic forces.

Messiness: 2
Prep Time: None
Activity Time: 15 minutes

MATERIALS

Various small household objects, such as paper clips, pom-poms, spoons, coins, crumpled-up paper, crumpled-up aluminum foil, letter magnets, and plastic animal toys (about half of them should have magnetic properties)

Large shallow plastic bin

2 dining chairs

Magnetic wand or other strong magnet

STEPS

1. Together with your toddler, go on a hunt around the house for various small objects. Choose both magnetic and nonmagnetic objects, but don't tell your child which are which. Gather them in the plastic bin as you go.

2. Place the bin on both dining chairs so that each chair is supporting one end of the bin. The majority of the bin's bottom should be accessible to your toddler. Move the household objects to one end of the bin.

3. Demonstrate how to use the magnetic wand under the bottom of the bin by using it to move one of the magnetic objects to the other side of the bin. Explain magnetism as a force that pulls certain objects—usually metal ones—together.

4. Now it's your toddler's turn! Using the wand, have her experiment to see which of the other objects in the bin are magnetic. Which ones can she use the wand to move to the other side of the bin?

NEXT LEVEL: If you have some letter magnets, you can pop those in the shallow bin. First, use dry-erase markers to draw different-color circles on the bottom of the bin, each corresponding to the color of one of the letter magnets. Then put the letter magnets in the bin and invite your toddler to use the magnetic wand to move each magnet to its matching-color circle. Or challenge an older child to locate and position the letters of her name by using the magnetic wand with the magnetic letters.

CAUTION! Supervise your toddler during play and never leave the activity set up and unsupervised, as the materials can be a choking and injury hazard.

COLORS

FINE MOTOR
SKILLS

SOCIAL-EMOTIONAL
DEVELOPMENT

SORTING

VISUAL SPATIAL
SKILLS

Colorful Eyes and Emotions Snack

This simple fine motor activity offers color-matching practice and social-emotional learning—all using tasty O-shaped cereal!

Messiness: 2
Prep Time: **None**
Activity Time: **15 minutes**

MATERIALS

Washable markers that match the colors of the cereal

White paper

Colorful O-shaped cereal, placed in a container

STEPS

1. Draw different-colored circles all over the paper. Add dots for eyes and lines for mouths, and make each face express a different emotion.

2. Invite your child to choose one face, identify its color, and then place matching-color O-shaped cereal pieces over the drawn eyes. Talk about the emotion of the face.

3. Repeat until each face has O-shaped cereal eyes.

AGE ADAPTATION: If it's all you have, or if your toddler isn't ready for color sorting, use plain O-shaped cereal and focus on positioning the pieces on the dot eyes and identifying the emotions.

CAUTION! Monitor your toddler closely when playing with small objects.

Suction Shape Sort

Blowing and sucking through a straw provides oral motor skill practice and sensory regulation. Top that with some shape sorting and you'll have a comprehensive toddler activity that is, first and foremost, fun!

Messiness: 2
Prep Time: None
Activity Time: 10 minutes

MATERIALS

6 different shapes
of craft foam shapes,
in multiples

6-cup muffin pan

Straw

CAUTION! Make sure all shapes are larger than the end of the straw so they cannot be sucked up through the straw and possibly be choked on. Monitor your toddler closely when playing with small objects. This activity may not be suitable for children who put objects in their mouths during play.

STEPS

1. Have your toddler help you place one of each different foam shape in the bottom of each cup of the muffin pan. Identify each shape and color while doing so.

2. Scatter the rest of the foam shapes on a flat surface.

3. Demonstrate how to use a straw to pick up each shape: place one end of the straw in your mouth and place the other end on a shape. Then suck through the straw and the shape sticks to it! Still sucking through the straw, transfer the foam shape to its muffin pan cup with the matching shape.

4. Allow your toddler to try it and let her continue practicing until all the shapes have been sorted into the cups with their matching shapes.

SIMPLE SWAP: No craft foam shapes? Cut simple squares out of different-colored construction paper and have your toddler sort them by color. Or, cut stickers apart and have her transfer those. If you have multiples of each sticker, have her sort them by type.

ORAL MOTOR
DEVELOPMENT

SENSORY
DEVELOPMENT

SHAPES AND
LETTERS

SORTING

Coin Squish Patterns

FINE MOTOR
SKILLS

123

NUMBERS AND
COUNTING

SENSORY
DEVELOPMENT

SORTING

Get your little one exploring coins and building early math skills with this toddler playdough activity.

Messiness: **3**
Prep Time: **None**
Activity Time: **15 minutes**

MATERIALS

Various coins, including pennies, nickels, dimes, and quarters

4 small plastic food storage containers

Playdough, store-bought or using recipe on page 44

STEPS

1. Discuss the coins and their values while your toddler examines them. Have him place a penny in one container, a nickel in the second container, a dime in the third container, and a quarter in the last one. Encourage him to sort the remaining coins into their matching coin containers.

2. Help your toddler make a long snake of play-dough. Place it on the table, then show him how to squish the coins into it. Invite him to take over the coin squishing!

3. Ask your toddler to try making simple patterns with the coins in the playdough snakes, such as an ABA pattern (penny, dime, penny, dime . . .) or an ABBA pattern (penny, dime, dime, penny . . .).

SIMPLE SWAP: No playdough? No problem! Just make the coin patterns in rows along the table.

CAUTION! Monitor your toddler closely when playing with small objects. This activity may not be suitable for children who put objects in their mouths during play.

Coffee Filter Color-Mixing

Grab a coffee filter from the cupboard for a quick colorful science experiment your toddler is sure to love.

SKILLS LEARNED

COLORS

FINE MOTOR SKILLS

SCIENCE

Messiness: 3
Prep Time: None
Activity Time: 10 minutes

MATERIALS

White coffee filter, any size

Flat tray

Washable markers in red, yellow, and blue

Cup with water

STEPS

1. Flatten the coffee filter out into a circle on the tray. Use one of the markers to put a dot in the approximate center of it.

2. Have your toddler help draw many red, yellow, and blue lines, starting at the dot and going out to the edge of the coffee filter.

3. With the marker-side out, fold the coffee filter in half, then in quarters, and again in eighths, until it is a small wedge-like triangle. Place it in the cup of water so the point just touches the water.

4. Encourage your toddler to watch as the coffee filter absorbs the water, and talk about what the water does to the marker colors. If any new colors appear where the marker lines run together, help your child identify them.

5. Take your colorful coffee filter out of the cup and lay flat to dry.

NEXT LEVEL: Once your colorful coffee filter is dry, allow your little one to draw on it with a black marker. Then tape it onto a window as a colorful suncatcher.

LANGUAGE DEVELOPMENT

123
NUMBERS AND COUNTING

PROBLEM-SOLVING

SCIENCE

Toy Weigh Station

Let your little one explore the science of gravity and the measurement of weight with a basic bathroom scale.

Messiness: 2
Prep Time: **None**
Activity Time: **15 minutes**

MATERIALS

Various toys of different weights

Bathroom scale

Plastic pail or basket

STEPS

1. Together with your toddler, gather toys of different weights. Compare how heavy they feel while collecting them.

2. Have your toddler stand on the bathroom scale and help her identify the numbers on it.

3. Have your toddler hold the pail and see if the number on the scale increases. Then, have her choose a toy for you to put inside the pail she's holding. Observe and discuss how the weight on the scale changes.

4. Repeat until all of the toys have been weighed. Try determining which toy weighs the most and which weighs the least.

5. Encourage lots of number identification and talk about the measurement of weight using terms like *light, heavy, least, most, less, and more.*

SIMPLE SWAP: No bathroom scale? A kitchen scale could also work for weighing small toys if you use a plastic food storage container to hold them.

Cloud Dough Name Puzzle

This homemade sensory material is a toddler-friendly favorite. It requires only two ingredients from the pantry, some fun shaking to make it, and is taste-safe for curious little ones.

Messiness: **4**
Prep Time: **None**
Activity Time: **20 minutes**

MATERIALS

8 cups flour

1 cup cooking oil, any kind

Large plastic food storage container with a tight lid

Medium-size shallow plastic bin

Foam bath letters, letter magnets, or washable letter puzzle pieces

STEPS

1. Put the flour and cooking oil in the plastic food storage container and make sure to tightly secure the lid. Have your toddler help shake the container to thoroughly mix the ingredients inside.

2. Remove the lid and check the consistency of the "cloud dough" with your hands. Add more oil or flour as needed, and shake, until the dough reaches a soft consistency that holds together when squeezed. Pour it into the shallow plastic bin.

3. Have your toddler press each letter of his name into the cloud dough, then remove it, creating an impression of his name in the dough.

4. Randomly place the letters he used around the impression of his name. Challenge him to match the letters to their impressions, like a puzzle.

SIMPLE SWAP: If you don't have any letters, try using any wooden chunky puzzle pieces, building blocks of various shapes, or even plastic animal toys. Free play with any washable toys in the cloud dough can be fun, too.

CAUTION! While this homemade cloud dough is taste-safe for curious toddlers, it is not intended for eating.

EARLY LITERACY

SENSORY DEVELOPMENT

SHAPES AND LETTERS

Baby Gate Snakes

With a baby gate and a little imagination, this fun activity will have your child practicing her fine motor skills and strengthening her oral motor development.

Messiness: **2**
Prep Time: **None**
Activity Time: **20 minutes**

MATERIALS

Baby gate

Various ribbons, belts, and lightweight scarves

STEPS

1. Sit on one side of the baby gate while your toddler sits on the other.

2. Choose one ribbon, belt, or scarf, and thread one end of it through a hole in the baby gate. Tell your toddler it's a friendly snake and make a hissing sound.

3. Tell her to take the end of the snake and thread it back through a different hole. (You may need to reach over the top of the gate to help her until she gets the hang of it.) Be sure you both make lots of friendly hissing sounds.

4. Thread the material back and forth, weaving it into the gate. Repeat, with different ribbons, belts, and scarves, and more silly snake hissing.

AGE ADAPTATION: Older toddlers and big kids might enjoy weaving the materials in rows and patterns to make a creative art piece.

CAUTION! Supervise your toddler during play and never leave the activity set up and unsupervised, as the materials can be a strangulation and injury hazard.

Nesting Bowl Size Sort

Grab some bowls from the kitchen for a simple but fun way to explore size and make comparisons with your toddler.

Messiness: **1**
Prep Time: **None**
Activity Time: **10 minutes**

MATERIALS

3 or more nesting mixing bowls

Toys of various sizes

STEPS

1. Present the bowls to your toddler and discuss their size. Use words like *small, medium,* and *large,* as well as *smaller, smallest, larger,* and *largest.*

2. Have your toddler find a toy that will fit in each bowl. Encourage him to try different toys in the different bowls.

3. Challenge him to sort the toys by size from smallest to largest.

NEXT LEVEL: Add some fun early math learning by having your toddler fill each bowl with building blocks and asking him to count how many blocks each bowl will hold.

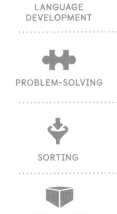

SKILLS LEARNED

LANGUAGE DEVELOPMENT

PROBLEM-SOLVING

SORTING

VISUAL SPATIAL SKILLS

SCIENCE

SENSORY
DEVELOPMENT

SHAPES AND
LETTERS

VISUAL SPATIAL
SKILLS

Squishy Shapes Sensory Bag

Zip-top bags are a great sensory activity tool for toddlers, especially because they keep any mess contained! Here's a super simple squishy shapes game for your little one to play.

Messiness: **1**
Prep Time: **5 minutes**
Activity Time: **10 minutes**

MATERIALS

1 cup baby oil or cooking oil

1 cup water, colored with food coloring

Craft foam shapes

Gallon-size zip-top bag

Duct tape

PREP

Add the oil, colored water, and craft foam shapes to the bag. Seal the bag tightly and cover the sealed edge with duct tape for extra security.

STEPS

1. Lay the bag flat on the table and invite your child to poke and squish the bag with her fingers to explore the oil, water, and shapes inside.

2. Encourage her to notice how the oil and water react to one another and do not mix.

3. Challenge her by calling out certain shapes for her to find—and squish!—with her fingers.

SIMPLE SWAP: You can vary the kinds of craft foam shapes you use to customize the learning. For example, you might use letters, then numbers, then shapes. Or, if you don't have any craft foam at all, try using different-color beads, buttons, or sequins and call out colors for your child to find.

CAUTION! Supervise your toddler during play and never leave the activity set up and unsupervised, as the materials can be a choking hazard.

Fingerprint Alphabet Song

Try this simple activity to add a hands-on sensory element to your toddler's alphabet song singing.

Messiness: **3**
Prep Time: **None**
Activity Time: **10 minutes**

MATERIALS

Black permanent marker

White paper

Ink pad with washable ink or washable paint in a bowl

STEPS

1. Sing the alphabet song with your toddler, reviewing the letters of the alphabet, while you write the letters of the alphabet in a long winding line on the piece of paper.

2. Invite your toddler to press a finger into the ink pad and then press that finger onto each letter of the alphabet, beginning with the letter A, as you sing the alphabet song together.

3. Have your toddler press a finger into the ink pad as needed to make clear fingerprints on each letter.

AGE ADAPTATION: For an older child, write the letters randomly on the paper and call out letters for him to find and cover with his fingerprint.

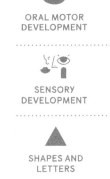

DIY Grocery Spy Game

EARLY LITERACY

VISUAL SPATIAL SKILLS

When my kids were challenging little shoppers, I came up with this easy game to keep them entertained at the grocery store. Try it with your little shopper!

Messiness: **1**
Prep Time: **5 minutes**
Activity Time: **15 minutes**

MATERIALS

Scissors

Empty food boxes, such as cereal, mac and cheese, and pasta

Hole punch

Metal binder ring

PREP

1. At home, use scissors to cut the brand names and/or the names of the food from empty food boxes, making each into a four- to six-inch square or rectangle.

2. Punch a hole in the corner of each square/ rectangle and thread them all onto the binder ring.

STEPS

1. Give your toddler the ring while grocery shopping. Help her identify each food item while flipping through the squares/rectangles on the binder ring.

2. Challenge her to try to spy each food item in the store while shopping.

3. Add to the learning by asking which meal the foods are good for, such as *"What meal do we eat cereal for?"* Or, discuss the different food groups while shopping.

SIMPLE SWAP: If you don't have a binder ring, you could thread a piece of string through the punched holes and tie everything loosely together. Or, you could slide the cut-out squares/rectangles into a mini photo book for your toddler to flip through at the store.

Back Shapes Game

Since it requires no materials, this simple learning game can even be played while you and your toddler are waiting in a restaurant or standing in an amusement park line.

SENSORY DEVELOPMENT

SHAPES AND LETTERS

Messiness: 0
Prep Time: None
Activity Time: 10 minutes

MATERIALS

Nothing!

STEPS

1. Review the basic shapes with your toddler and use a finger to draw each one in the air or on a surface.

2. Have your child sit or stand with his back facing you. Use your index finger to draw a basic shape (circle, square, rectangle, triangle, oval, or diamond) on his back. Challenge him to guess which shape it is. Draw it again, more slowly, if he is not able to tell you what shape it is.

3. Repeat, until you have done each shape. Then turn your back to your toddler so he can have fun drawing shapes on your back for you to guess!

AGE ADAPTATION: Adapt the learning for your toddler by trying this same game using letters of the alphabet or numbers instead. Consider drawing more elaborate pictures or entire words for older children to guess.

COLORS

CREATIVITY

FINE MOTOR
SKILLS

SENSORY
DEVELOPMENT

VISUAL SPATIAL
SKILLS

Rubber Bands and Blocks Play

Toddlers love exploring stretchy rubber bands. Plus, the resistance of rubber bands offers extra fine motor skill strengthening for little fingers.

Messiness: 2
Prep Time: **Less than 5 minutes**
Activity Time: **15 minutes**

MATERIALS

Rubber bands, ideally in colors that match the blocks

LEGO Duplo blocks or other toy building blocks

PREP

Place rubber bands around various blocks. Place these blocks alongside the rest of the blocks and rubber bands.

STEPS

1. Invite your child to play freely and creatively with all the blocks and rubber bands.

2. Challenge her to try to remove the rubber bands you already placed on blocks.

3. If you have colored rubber bands, challenge your toddler to place rubber bands on matching-color blocks.

CAUTION! Supervise your toddler during play and never leave the materials set up and unsupervised, as they can be a choking and injury hazard.

NEXT LEVEL: If you have craft sticks, especially colored ones, provide some for creative play and building fun along with the blocks and rubber bands. Show your toddler how the sticks can be slid underneath the rubber bands that are around blocks to attach them to the blocks.

Dish Drainer Clip Game

The act of clipping clothespins provides toddlers with lots of fine motor and hand-eye coordination practice. Here's a clever clip game using a common kitchen item!

Messiness: 2
Prep Time: Less than 5 minutes
Activity Time: 15 minutes

MATERIALS

Dice

Sealable clear plastic food storage container

Dish drainer

Clothespins

PREP

Place the dice in the sealable clear plastic food storage container. Turn the dish drainer upside down and put it somewhere easy for your toddler to reach it.

STEPS

1. Invite your toddler to shake the container with the dice. Look through the clear container and help him count the dots on the dice.

2. Ask your toddler to count and clip the same number of clothespins onto one of the wires or edges of the dish drainer.

3. Encourage your child to repeat until all the clothespins have been clipped.

SIMPLE SWAP: No dish drainer? Use a large plastic food storage container or cooking stockpot, and have your toddler clip clothespins around the edges of that.

CAUTION! Monitor your toddler closely when playing with small objects. This activity may not be suitable for children who put objects in their mouths during play.

SKILLS LEARNED

FINE MOTOR SKILLS

123
NUMBERS AND COUNTING

VISUAL SPATIAL SKILLS

Road Trip Phone Game

Play this pretend phone conversation game when you're on a long road trip, or just simply to keep your toddler learning while running errands around town.

Messiness: 0
Prep Time: None
Activity Time: 10 minutes

MATERIALS

Nothing!

STEPS

1. Place your hand up to your ear as if you are using a pretend cell phone. Make a ringing sound and pretend to call your toddler. Encourage her to answer with her own pretend cell phone.

2. When she answers, model polite phone conversation, such as, *"Hello, [Name]! How are you today?"* Then, tell her you're riding in a car on the road and tell her three things you see outside your window.

3. End the pretend phone conversation politely, saying something like, *"It was so nice talking to you, [Name]. Bye now."*

4. Then have your toddler pretend to call you and give you her own road trip update, telling you three things she sees outside her window. Encourage polite conversation during her call.

NEXT LEVEL: Add to the challenge and fun by asking your child to call you back when she sees something on her trip that is a certain color.

Bathtub Pouring Practice

Set up this simple play activity right in the bathtub to give your toddler hands-on learning through pouring practice.

SENSORY DEVELOPMENT

VISUAL SPATIAL SKILLS

Messiness: **3**
Prep Time: **None**
Activity Time: **15 minutes**

MATERIALS

Plastic cups, pitchers, and containers, in various sizes

Medium-size plastic bin

Bathtub

Water

STEPS

1. Together with your toddler, gather up various plastic cups, containers, and pitchers and place them in the medium-size plastic bin. Then place the bin in the bathtub.

2. Help your toddler into the bathtub and have him take everything out of the bin. Fill the bin with water.

3. Invite him to explore the various cups, pitchers, and containers, along with the water in the bin. Have him line up the different-size cups or containers along the floor of the bathtub, then ask him to use a pitcher or a larger container to pour water into each of them. Encourage him to notice how different sizes of containers hold different amounts of water.

NEXT LEVEL: Add to the fun and learning by using food coloring to color certain containers of water different primary colors (red, yellow, and blue). Encourage your child to identify the colors made when he mixes different colors of water together.

10

Ways to Entertain Your Toddler While Grocery Shopping

1. **Spy the Alphabet:** Try to find each letter of the alphabet, in order, on food labels or on signs around the store.

2. **Count at Checkout:** Count your items together as you place each one on the conveyor belt at checkout.

3. **Color Point:** Choose a color for her to point to each time she spots it in the store.

4. **Store Flyer Picnic:** Grab the store flyer on your way in and let your toddler circle items he would want for the ultimate imaginary picnic.

5. **Imaginative Shopping Fun:** Have your toddler choose a dress-up item to wear while shopping and engage in imaginative play as you make your way through the store. For example, your child could have a superhero cape (for being your super-helper), a fairy wand (for pointing at items as you find them), or be wearing a crown (for finding items that someone royal would like to eat).

6. **Flashcard Practice:** Punch holes in flashcards and put them on a binder ring to take along and practice.

7. **Grocery Store Simon Says:** Play Simon Says using only upper body movement and speech commands, such as "touch your nose" or "say your name."

8. **Tap Back:** Tap a beat on the shopping cart for your toddler to mimic and tap back.

9. **Help Carry:** Allow him to gather items and put them in the cart, especially heavier items that can have a calming sensory effect.

10. **Silly Story Game:** Start a story with a random line, then have your toddler add a line to the story. Add another line to the story and go back and forth to create a long silly story.

4
Get Creative

Opportunities to practice developing motor skills abound in creative toddler activities. The skills and activities range from strengthening fine motor skills by cutting paper and coloring with markers to honing coordination and gross motor skills by practicing new dance skills—and there's so much more! Creativity is also vital for your toddler's growing brain and budding independence. By engaging in creative activities, such as art projects, baking cookies, or dancing, your toddler gets to experiment, problem-solve, and express themselves.

I know what you're thinking . . . *"Oh no. Arts and crafts are so messy."* But don't worry. I've designed the following creative activities to be simple to do and easy to clean up, while still providing all of the benefits of creativity for your little one.

CREATIVITY

FINE MOTOR
SKILLS

GROSS MOTOR
SKILLS

Rainbow Streamer Ring

Add some movement and creativity to your toddler's favorite music by making a colorful streamer ring! He can take his streamer ring outside on a windy day, as well, for hands-on weather learning.

Messiness: **1**
Prep Time: **None**
Activity Time: **15 minutes**

MATERIALS

Safety scissors

Various string-like materials, such as ribbon, yarn, and crepe paper streamers, in various colors of the rainbow

Canning jar band

Music

STEPS

1. Allow your toddler to get scissor practice while helping you cut various two- to three-foot lengths of ribbon, string, or streamers.

2. Tie each ribbon and streamer onto the canning jar band.

3. Put on your toddler's favorite music and encourage him to hold and move the streamer ring while dancing and moving to the music.

SIMPLE SWAP: No canning jar band? You could use a metal binder ring, shower curtain ring, or old teething ring instead. Or, tie the streamers through the slots of a plastic spatula to make a streamer wand.

CAUTION! Supervise your toddler closely when he is using the safety scissors.

Sticky Squares and Rectangles

My J.C. went through a sticky note phase. He was fascinated with sticky notes of all kinds, and loved sticking them all over the house. Keep the sticky notes off your walls by having your toddler create some abstract shape-filled art instead!

Messiness: **1**
Prep Time: **None**
Activity Time: **10 minutes**

MATERIALS

Sticky notes in various colors and sizes

Sticky flags in various colors and sizes

White paper

STEPS

1. Invite your toddler to explore the sticky notes and flags. Help him identify their colors and shapes (rectangles and squares).

2. Explain that abstract art is art made with shapes, lines, colors, and more, but a piece of abstract art doesn't have any recognizable objects in it. Encourage your toddler to make his own piece of abstract art by placing sticky notes and flags wherever he wants to on the paper!

NEXT LEVEL: Take your square and rectangle art to the next level by allowing your child to add lines and patterns to it with a black marker.

SKILLS LEARNED

COLORS

CREATIVITY

FINE MOTOR SKILLS

SHAPES AND LETTERS

Wheels on the Bin Bus

CREATIVITY

IMAGINATION

LANGUAGE
DEVELOPMENT

ORAL MOTOR
DEVELOPMENT

What toddler doesn't love the "Wheels on the Bus" song? With a couple of household items, you can have your toddler driving her very own bus while she sings and plays.

Messiness: **1**
Prep Time: **None**
Activity Time: **10 minutes**

MATERIALS

Crayons

5 sturdy paper plates

Large plastic bin
or large rectangular
cardboard box

Tape

Stuffed animals

STEPS

1. Have your toddler help color the bottom of four of the paper plates with a black crayon. Tape the plates, black side out, onto the sides of the bin to be the wheels of the school bus.

2. Allow her to color the fifth paper plate with any color crayon she desires. Help her into the bin bus and ask her to sit near one end. Give her the fifth paper plate to hold and turn like a steering wheel. She's going to be a bus driver!

3. Grab some stuffed animals to be bus passengers and place them in the bin behind your toddler driver. Sing "The Wheels on the Bus" and encourage your toddler to move like the bus parts do in the song:

    - *The wheels on the bus go 'round and 'round:* Have your child point at each wheel on her bus and make circular motions.
    - *The door on the bus goes open and shut:* Have your child move her right arm out and back in as if opening and shutting the bus door. Help the stuffed animals pretend to get off and on the bus.
    - *The wipers on the bus go swish, swish, swish:* Have your toddler hold both arms up, bend them at the elbows, and move them like windshield wipers.

- *The people on the bus go up and down:* **Move the stuffed animal passengers up and down as if they are having a bumpy bus ride.**
- *The horn on the bus goes beep, beep, beep:* **Have your child hold the steering wheel in one hand while using her other hand to honk a pretend horn in the middle of the steering wheel. Invite her to shout,** *"Beep, beep, beep!"*
- *The driver on the bus says "Move on back!":* **Have your toddler turn her head to look over her shoulder and point behind her with one hand.**

NEXT LEVEL: If you have some construction paper and extra time, line the outside of the bin with yellow paper and add construction paper circles to the center of the plate wheels. Either way, you'll want to keep your box bus for lots more imaginative play!

Circle Celebration Mandala

CREATIVITY

FINE MOTOR
SKILLS

MINDFULNESS

PATTERNS

SHAPES AND
LETTERS

Circles have been revered throughout history as being symbolic of the universe, wholeness, and balance. In some cultures, circular designs are referred to as mandalas. Explore circles with your toddler by making this toddler-friendly mandala together, then use it to practice mindfulness.

Messiness: 1
Prep Time: None
Activity Time: 15 minutes

MATERIALS

Various circular objects for tracing, such as a roll of masking tape, bowls, and cups

White paper plate

Pencil

Colored dot labels in various colors

STEPS

1. Help your toddler choose the smallest circular object, then place it in the center of the paper plate and trace around it with a pencil. Invite her to choose one slightly larger circular object, place it in the center of the paper plate, and trace around it with a pencil. Repeat, tracing multiple concentric circles on the paper plate.

2. Invite your toddler to make designs on the paper plate by sticking dot labels on the circle lines.

3. Add to the learning by suggesting she make simple patterns, such as an ABA pattern (red dot, yellow dot, red dot . . .) or an ABBA pattern (red dot, yellow dot, yellow dot, red dot . . .) along the circle lines.

4. Explain how some people think creating and looking at circle designs can help a person relax and feel calm. Introduce and explain the word mandala. Try doing a short, simple meditation together by being quiet and focusing on the circle mandala.

SIMPLE SWAP: No dot labels? Use dot markers instead. No dot markers either? Use any kind of sticker to make designs around the circles.

Body Parts Dance Party

Try this fun and easy way to add some important body part learning to a creative dance activity.

Messiness: 0
Prep Time: None
Activity Time: 10 minutes

MATERIALS

Just music!

STEPS

1. Review the parts of the body, such as hand, leg, arm, foot, belly, and head, by helping your toddler point to each one and name them.

2. Challenge your toddler to identify specific body parts as you randomly call them out.

3. Put some music on, and have your toddler shake and move specific body parts to the music as you randomly call them out.

AGE ADAPTATION: Make it more challenging for older children by calling out two or more body parts at once or specifying left or right body parts.

CREATIVITY

GROSS MOTOR SKILLS

LANGUAGE DEVELOPMENT

LISTENING

SENSORY DEVELOPMENT

Fruit and Waffle Patterns

CREATIVITY

FINE MOTOR
SKILLS

PATTERNS

Playing with food is a favorite pastime of toddlerhood. It's actually quite beneficial for a toddler, too! This creative snack will have your toddler exploring various fruits, practicing his developing fine motor skills, and expanding his creativity. And, with this creative activity, your toddler will also be learning early math concepts—all while having a yummy snack, of course!

Messiness: **2**
Prep Time: **5 minutes**
Activity Time: **15 minutes**

MATERIALS

Frozen waffles

Paring knife

Variety of fruit, such as strawberries, blueberries, bananas, and kiwi

Containers or small bowls, one per fruit

Plastic plate and toddler fork

PREP

1. Prepare waffles according to the package directions.

2. Cut the fruit into pieces similar in size to the squares on the waffles.

3. Place each kind of fruit in its own bowl.

STEPS

1. Give your toddler a waffle (or two!) on a plate, and show him how to place pieces of fruit in the squares to make a design on his waffle.

2. Suggest he try making simple patterns with the fruit on his waffle, such as an ABA pattern (blueberry, banana, blueberry . . .) or an ABBA pattern (blueberry, banana, banana, blueberry . . .).

3. When he's done designing, cut the waffle and fruit into bite-size pieces so he can enjoy his masterpiece!

AGE ADAPTATION: For an older toddler or child, give him a butter knife so he can help cut up soft fruit, like bananas. You can also provide a toothpick for him to use to transfer the fruit pieces onto his waffle.

CAUTION! Keep your toddler away from sharp knives while you are using them. Monitor your toddler closely during the activity and while eating. This activity may not be suitable for children who cannot sufficiently chew these foods.

CREATIVITY

FINE MOTOR
SKILLS

SENSORY
DEVELOPMENT

Instant Office Supply Instruments

Playing instruments provides numerous creative benefits to toddlers. Raid your office supplies to make a few instruments for your very own toddler-friendly orchestra!

Messiness: **1**
Prep Time: **None**
Activity Time: **20 minutes**

MATERIALS

Rubber Band Guitar

Rubber bands

Large plastic food storage container

Paper Clip Shaker

Paper clips

Small plastic food storage container with lid

Tape (optional)

Drum and Pencil Drumsticks

Large plastic food storage container

2 unsharpened pencils

Binder Ring Tambourine

Sturdy paper plate

Hole punch

4 binder rings

RUBBER BAND GUITAR

1. Wrap multiple rubber bands around the large plastic container so they are positioned an inch apart across the open top.

2. Invite your little musician to pluck and strum the rubber bands so they make sounds.

PAPER CLIP SHAKER

1. Place paper clips inside the small plastic container and tightly secure the lid. Add tape to further secure the lid, if necessary.

2. Let your toddler *shake, shake, shake* the container so it makes noise.

DRUM AND PENCIL DRUMSTICKS

Turn a large plastic container upside down and give your little drummer two unsharpened pencils to use as drumsticks on the container.

BINDER RING TAMBOURINE

1. Every couple of inches around the edge of a sturdy paper plate, punch two holes that touch one another to make a larger hole. Hook two binder rings in each hole.

2. Hand the tambourine plate to your toddler and encourage them to shake it and play it!

NEXT LEVEL: Play a "Follow My Beat" game by making a beat with an instrument and challenging your child to repeat it back to you with her instrument.

CAUTION! Monitor your toddler closely when playing with small objects. This activity may not be suitable for children who put objects in their mouths during play.

CREATIVITY

FINE MOTOR
SKILLS

PATTERNS

VISUAL SPATIAL
SKILLS

Straw Bead Starburst Ornament

Your toddler will get loads of fine motor skill practice threading straw beads for this ornament craft. Bonus: She can give the finished starburst ornament to someone as a handmade gift, too!

Messiness: **2**
Prep Time: **None**
Activity Time: **15 minutes**

MATERIALS

Scissors, one pair regular and one pair safety

Straws in various colors

Pipe cleaners

String or thread

CAUTION! Keep your toddler away from sharp scissors while you are using them, and supervise her closely when she is using the safety scissors. Monitor your toddler closely when playing with small objects. This activity may not be suitable for children who put objects in their mouths during play.

STEPS

1. Use scissors to cut the straws into half-inch pieces to create straw "beads." Let your little one practice cutting a straw with safety scissors.

2. Twist two pipe cleaners together at the middle until they are secure. Add another pipe cleaner by twisting it around the middle of those. Repeat, attaching multiple pipe cleaners at the middle. Fan the pipe cleaner ends out to make a three-dimensional starburst design.

3. Invite your toddler to thread straw beads onto the pipe cleaners. Help her fold the ends of each pipe cleaner over the last bead and twist it onto itself like a knot, so all the beads will stay on the pipe cleaner.

4. Add to the learning by asking your child to thread the beads in patterns, such as an ABA pattern (blue, green, blue . . .) or an ABBA pattern (blue, green, green, blue . . .).

5. Tie some string to the starburst for hanging.

NEXT LEVEL: If you have any craft beads, use them instead of or with the straw beads.

Snip and Fold Flower

This cute flower craft offers tons of fine motor skill practice yet only requires a paper plate and a couple of art supplies. Plus, you wind up with a colorful flower you can hang to brighten up the house!

Messiness: 2
Prep Time: None
Activity Time: 20 minutes

MATERIALS

White paper plate, any size

Paper towels

Washable paint sticks

Safety scissors

Pencil (optional)

CAUTION! Monitor your toddler closely when he is using safety scissors.

STEPS

1. Invite your toddler to decorate the paper plate (which should be on top of paper towels) using paint sticks. Ask him to make the outside inch or so a different color from the inside of the plate.

2. Flip the plate over and ask him to color the outer edge on this side a different color from the other side. Allow a few minutes for the paint to dry, if needed.

3. By carefully using the safety scissors, help your toddler make snips around the edge of the plate, moving in toward the center of the plate, with each snip being about an inch apart from the others. If you like, before your toddler begins this step, you might make pencil marks to indicate exactly where he should be cutting. Help your toddler fold every other cut piece in toward the center of the flower.

4. Let some early science learning bloom by talking about the characteristics of flowers, such as how they grow from seeds using soil, sunlight, and water; how they typically grow in spring and summer; and how some animals and insects need flowers for food, water, and shelter.

SIMPLE SWAP: If you don't have paint sticks, you can use any other common kids' art supply item like crayons, washable paint, or markers.

CREATIVITY

FINE MOTOR SKILLS

SCIENCE

CREATIVITY

FINE MOTOR
SKILLS

VISUAL SPATIAL
SKILLS

Coloring Page Puzzle

Your toddler will get a kick out of having her very own puzzle made out of her own coloring art! And, you'll get a handy little puzzle to tuck in your purse for on-the-go fun.

Messiness: 1
Prep Time: None
Activity Time: 20 minutes

MATERIALS

Coloring book page, removed from the coloring book

Crayons

Glue stick

Card stock or cereal box cardboard

Scissors

STEPS

1. Allow your toddler to color the coloring book page any way she desires.

2. When she is done, flip the page over and have her help apply glue all over the back using a glue stick. Then, glue the page onto the piece of card stock.

3. Use scissors to cut the coloring page into four to six wavy or zigzag strips, which will be used like puzzle pieces

4. Mix the puzzle pieces up and have your toddler try putting the coloring page puzzle back together!

NEXT LEVEL: Place the puzzle pieces into a gallon-size zip-top storage bag to pop in your purse for quick fun while on the go.

CAUTION! Monitor your toddler closely when you are using sharp scissors.

Everyday Objects Sculpture

It only takes a few everyday items added to your toddler's play-dough time to inspire loads of problem-solving and creativity.

CREATIVITY

FINE MOTOR SKILLS

SENSORY DEVELOPMENT

VISUAL SPATIAL SKILLS

Messiness: **3**
Prep Time: **Less than 5 minutes**
Activity Time: **15 minutes**

MATERIALS

Scissors

Straws

Cardboard paper towel tube

Empty cereal box

Aluminum foil

Playdough, store-bought or using recipe on page 44

CAUTION! Monitor your toddler closely when playing with small objects. This activity may not be suitable for children who put objects in their mouths during play. Monitor your toddler closely when you are using sharp scissors.

PREP

1. Cut the straws and cardboard paper towel tube into various lengths.

2. Cut the empty cereal box into various basic shapes.

3. Roll pieces of aluminum foil into various-size balls.

STEPS

1. Give your toddler the playdough and the pieces of everyday objects you prepared. Allow him time to explore and build with the materials.

2. Roll a little ball of playdough and show your toddler that he can use it to stick two objects together. Encourage him to roll more little balls of playdough and stick more objects together.

3. Help him make a base of playdough and encourage him to use the materials he stuck together and stick them to the base, building up to make a sculpture.

4. Explain sculpture as a three-dimensional art piece that isn't simply flat. Imagine what his sculpture could represent while he creates it—could it be a mansion of the future or a new kind of space shuttle?

NEXT LEVEL: If you have air-dry clay, use that instead of playdough so you can keep your toddler's sculpture after it dries.

CREATIVITY

IMAGINATION

ORAL MOTOR
DEVELOPMENT

SENSORY
DEVELOPMENT

Animal A Cappella

This simple music activity will have your toddler practicing animal identification, strengthening oral motor skills, and composing her own silly music, too!

Messiness: **1**
Prep Time: **None**
Activity Time: **10 minutes**

MATERIALS

Various stuffed animals or animal toys

STEPS

1. Have your toddler help gather various stuffed animals or animal toys. Line them up on the floor and help her identify each animal and practice its sound.

2. Challenge her to make the appropriate animal sounds while you point to different animal toys.

3. Try making animal sound "music" by going faster, pointing at different animal toys while she calls out their animal sounds. Take turns being the composer (pointer) and music (animal sounds).

NEXT LEVEL: Have a group of kids or siblings? Have each child choose and hold an animal toy and make the appropriate animal sound when they are pointed to.

Teddy Bear Trail Mix

Trail mix was one of my go-to recipes when my kids were toddlers because it was so easy for them to help make—and shake! Try this trail mix recipe with your toddler.

Messiness: **2**
Prep Time: **None**
Activity Time: **10 minutes**

MATERIALS

Measuring cup

1 cup teddy bear graham cracker snacks

1 cup toddler-friendly cereal

1 cup of a sweet snack, such as mini marshmallows or chocolate chips

1 cup of a salty snack, such as mini pretzels, peanuts, or mini crackers

Large plastic food storage container with lid

STEPS

1. Help your toddler measure and add each ingredient to the storage container.

2. Secure the lid tightly on the container and let your little one shake it to mix up the trail mix.

3. Have some trail mix for a snack! During snack time, talk about the different tastes and textures of the various trail mix ingredients. Ask your toddler which one they like best!

SIMPLE SWAP: Swap out the teddy bear snacks for other fun snacks. For instance, make "Fish Tank Trail Mix" using fish-shaped crackers. Or use animal crackers to make "Zoo Food."

CAUTION! Monitor your toddler closely around small food items. This activity may not be suitable for children who cannot chew the ingredients sufficiently.

CREATIVITY

FINE MOTOR SKILLS

ORAL MOTOR DEVELOPMENT

SENSORY DEVELOPMENT

SKILLS
LEARNED

COLORS

CREATIVITY

FINE MOTOR
SKILLS

SENSORY
DEVELOPMENT

Finger Painting— Inside the Box!

Don't let the fear of a mess keep your little one from the fun and creativity of finger painting. Just keep the mess contained— in a box!

Messiness: 4
Prep Time: None
Activity Time: 20 minutes

MATERIALS

Cardboard box, large enough for your toddler to sit in, with top flaps removed

Old towels (optional)

Swimsuit (optional)

Finger paint in primary colors of red, yellow, and blue

3 small plastic food storage containers

STEPS

1. Place the box on the towel-lined floor of the bathroom, if possible. Help your child into her swimsuit, if desired, and help her get inside the box.

2. Add some paint to each container, and place the containers of paint inside the box with your toddler. Encourage her to finger paint all over the inside of the box, as well as on her arms, legs, and toes, if desired.

3. Talk about how the three primary colors make new colors when they mix with one another.

4. When she's all done painting, help your toddler out of the box and right into the bathtub!

SIMPLE SWAP: Still not up for the finger painting mess? Let your little one get creative with washable markers or crayons inside the box instead.

Card and Cup Houses

Remember carefully stacking playing cards into tall towers and houses when you were a kid? Add some playdough to make it a fun toddler-friendly version.

Messiness: **3**
Prep Time: **None**
Activity Time: **15 minutes**

MATERIALS

Playdough, store-bought or using recipe on page 44

Plastic party cups, ideally in various colors and sizes

Playing cards

STEPS

1. Place the playdough, cups, and playing cards on a washable (or covered), flat surface. Challenge your toddler to use the materials to build a mansion.

2. Show her how to place small balls of playdough between cups and cards to hold them together.

3. Have an imaginative conversation about the mansion while she is building it, asking her what types of rooms it has and who lives there.

AGE ADAPTATION: Have an older child try building a mansion by balancing cups and playing cards without any playdough.

CAUTION! This activity may not be suitable for children who put objects in their mouths during play.

Color Fruit Pops

COLORS

FINE MOTOR
SKILLS

LANGUAGE
DEVELOPMENT

ORAL MOTOR
DEVELOPMENT

SENSORY
DEVELOPMENT

Here's a yummy way to explore different fruits and practice colors, too! Plus, your little one gets great fine motor practice making these pops.

Messiness: **3**
Prep Time: **5 minutes**
Activity Time: **15 minutes**

MATERIALS

Paring knife

Various fruits, such as strawberries, blueberries, bananas, kiwi, and raspberries

Ice cube tray

Tablespoon

Large container vanilla yogurt

Aluminum foil

Craft sticks

PREP

Peel the fruits, if needed. Chop each fruit up, and fill each space in the ice cube tray about halfway with one kind of fruit.

STEPS

1. Together with your toddler, look at and talk about the various fruits in the ice cube tray. Help him identify each fruit's color.

2. Call out a color for him to find in the ice cube tray. Have him call out the color and fruit, and then use the tablespoon to fill those spaces with yogurt.

3. Repeat until all ice cube spaces have been filled with yogurt. Give the tray a couple of taps on the table to settle the yogurt, and add more, if needed.

4. Cover the tray with aluminum foil. Then have your child help punch a craft stick through the foil into each ice cube space. Place the tray in the freezer for six hours, or until fully frozen. Then it's time to enjoy your color fruit pops!

NEXT LEVEL: If you have more time and want more colorful yogurt pops, add food coloring to make some yogurt the same color as each fruit color. Then, have your toddler match the yogurt to the same-color fruit in the tray when scooping it.

CAUTION! Monitor your toddler closely around small food items. This activity may not be suitable for children who cannot chew the ingredients sufficiently.

CREATIVITY

FINE MOTOR
SKILLS

SOCIAL-EMOTIONAL
DEVELOPMENT

Sunshine Photo Keepsake

I always sang a sunshine song to my kids when they were little. My Priscilla still hums it to herself to cheer up. Try singing with your toddler while you make this sweet sunshine keepsake together.

Messiness: 3
Prep Time: None
Activity Time: 15 minutes

MATERIALS

Paint sticks
or crayons

Photo of your
child's face

Small paper plate, white

Glue stick

Yellow sticky note flags

STEPS

1. Allow your toddler to decorate the paper plate with yellow and orange paint sticks.

2. Help your child glue the photo onto the center of the plate.

3. Add some glue around the edge of the plate. Have your toddler add sticky note flags around it, overhanging the plate's edge slightly, so the sticky note flags look like sun rays.

NEXT LEVEL: If you also have orange sticky note flags, you can add some learning by asking your child to create a simple pattern of yellow and orange sticky note flags around the plate's edge.

Shape Sponge Stamping

Kitchen sponges make great stampers. Cut some into basic shapes to inspire shape learning and creativity in your little one.

Messiness: **3**
Prep Time: **5 minutes**
Activity Time: **15 minutes**

MATERIALS

Scissors

2 or 3 sponges

Washable paint, each color in its own bowl

White paper

PREP

Cut the sponges into various basic shapes. Place each shape sponge next to its own color of paint in a bowl.

STEPS

1. Review the different shapes and paint colors with your toddler.

2. Demonstrate how to stamp with a sponge by dipping it in its paint and then pressing it onto the paper.

3. Encourage her to stamp different shape sponges onto the paper. Allow your little one to stamp shapes freely and creatively. You might also ask her to try making lines of shapes or simple patterns, such as an ABA pattern (red circle, yellow square, red circle . . .) or an ABBA pattern (red circle, yellow square, yellow square, red circle . . .).

AGE ADAPTATION: For an older child, consider using a ruler and pencil to lightly draw horizontal lines on which she can create shape patterns.

CAUTION! Monitor your toddler closely when you are using sharp scissors.

CREATIVITY

FINE MOTOR SKILLS

PATTERNS

SENSORY DEVELOPMENT

CREATIVITY

FINE MOTOR SKILLS

IMAGINATION

LANGUAGE DEVELOPMENT

Silly Glove Puppets

Have you ever noticed that it seems like your toddler listens more carefully to a puppet than to you? Make a puppet with your child to put on an imaginative puppet show, or to get your toddler's attention when it's time to clean up toys!

Messiness: **2**
Prep Time: **None**
Activity Time: **20 minutes**

MATERIALS

Rubber cleaning gloves

Self-adhesive googly eyes

Permanent markers

Stickers

STEPS

1. Put a glove on and hold your thumb and fingers together, as if making your hand talk. Have your toddler help put googly eyes on the glove along the side of the pointer finger.

2. Use permanent markers to draw lips on the sides of your gloved pointer finger and thumb. Draw on nostrils and any other details you would like.

3. Allow your toddler to decorate the puppet with stickers. It may be easier to take the glove off for this step.

4. Repeat steps 1–3 to make another puppet, if possible. Then, have your toddler help name each puppet and use them to put on a puppet show, encouraging language development and practicing manners.

NEXT LEVEL: If you have the time and materials, add hair to your puppet by gluing yarn or strips of felt onto the knuckle area of the glove.

CAUTION! Monitor your toddler closely when creating with small objects like googly eyes. This activity may not be suitable for children who put objects in their mouths during play.

Kitchen Sink Paint and Print

Here's another easy way for your toddler to enjoy the fun of painting without the mess. Go ahead and let your little one paint—inside the sink!

CREATIVITY

FINE MOTOR
SKILLS

SENSORY
DEVELOPMENT

Messiness: **4**
Prep Time: **None**
Activity Time: **20 minutes**

MATERIALS

Sink and stepstool

Washable paint

Paintbrush

White paper

STEPS

1. Help your toddler up onto a stepstool positioned at the sink. Ask him what colors of paint he would like to use and squirt some right into the bottom of the sink. Encourage him to use the paintbrush and paint to paint all over the inside of the sink.

2. Help him make a print of his sink painting by pressing a piece of paper onto a section of the painted sink area, and then pulling the paper off to see the print. Set the paper aside to dry.

3. Repeat, allowing him to continue painting and helping him make prints.

AGE ADAPTATION: For an older toddler, add more learning by challenging him to finger paint letters, numbers, or shapes in the sink. Try printing them and notice how the letters and numbers come out backward on the print.

CAUTION! Supervise your toddler while he is on the stepstool. Never leave it set up when not supervising, as it can be a fall and injury hazard.

10
Everyday Items to Include in a Toddler Art Kit

1. **Kitchen Sponge:** Squirt paint on a sponge to use it as a stamper.

2. **Aluminum Foil:** Paint on foil with kids' paint to make some shiny art.

3. **Zip-Top Bags:** Seal a piece of paper and some paint inside for mess-free finger painting.

4. **Cotton Swabs:** Use them for painting dots or lines.

5. **Salt Shaker:** Sprinkle salt onto a wet watercolor painting and see what happens!

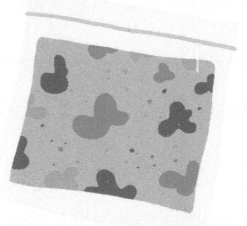

6. **Dish Brush:** You can use it instead of a paintbrush.

7. **Sticky Contact Paper:** Make a tissue paper collage on the sticky side.

8. **Cotton Balls:** Glue them down on artwork to create clouds or to add texture.

9. **Spray Bottle:** Fill it with water and food coloring to make spray paint.

10. **Clothespin:** Clip a pom-pom or small sponge in the end to use as a paint stamper.

* 5 *
Let's Pretend

My favorite part of toddler parenting is watching a toddler shift from focusing on motor skills and learning about the world to exploring self-expression and pretend play. Sure, it's awesome to see your little one discover something new in their world, but it's downright magical when they start creating that world right out of their own imagination!

The activities ahead each include a fun imaginative element. However, I urge you to leave room in each activity for your toddler's own ideas. Give them time to explore materials independently, prompt them to problem-solve and brainstorm, and gently guide them using the steps and tips as needed. I've tried to get my mind into toddler mode to think of imaginative uses of materials, but your toddler might have some even better ideas!

Super-Kindness Cuffs

CREATIVITY

FINE MOTOR
SKILLS

IMAGINATION

SOCIAL-EMOTIONAL
DEVELOPMENT

This simple craft and a little bit of imagination will have your toddler learning social-emotional skills and practicing random acts of kindness.

Messiness: **2**
Prep Time: **5 minutes**
Activity Time: **15 minutes**

MATERIALS

Scissors

Cardboard paper towel tube

Washable markers

Stickers, ideally stars and hearts

PREP

Cut down the length of the paper tube, then cut off two three-inch-wide pieces to make two cuffs.

STEPS

1. Invite your toddler to decorate the outside of the cardboard paper towel tube cuffs with markers and stickers.

2. Tell her they are magical superhero cuffs that give the person wearing them the superpower of being especially kind. Talk about the meaning of kindness and brainstorm acts of kindness together, such as smiling at someone, giving someone a compliment, or sharing a toy.

3. When your toddler is done making her cuffs, help her put one on each arm and go practice some random acts of kindness!

NEXT LEVEL: If you have glue and glitter or self-adhesive rhinestones, consider adding some shine to your super-kindness cuffs.

CAUTION! Monitor your toddler closely when you are using sharp scissors.

Water-Free Car Wash

What better way to use all of the streamers and balloons after a birthday party than to make a toddler-size car wash?

Messiness: **2**
Prep Time: **5 minutes**
Activity Time: **10 minutes**

MATERIALS

Tape

String

Indoor ride-on toy

Crepe paper party streamers, ideally in blue and/or white

Balloons, ideally in blue and/or white, inflated

Hand towel (optional)

PREP

1. Tape a string horizontally across a doorway high enough so your toddler can ride safely under it with his ride-on toy.

2. Tie or tape streamers along the string; they should end about a foot from the floor.

3. Place inflated balloons on the floor around the streamers.

STEPS

1. Invite your child to ride his ride-on toy through the streamers as if it's a pretend car wash. Make lots of car wash sounds!

2. If you have a towel, pretend to dry off his ride-on toy after he comes through the car wash.

3. Continue allowing your child to go through the car wash for as long as he is interested in doing so.

NEXT LEVEL: If you have a fan, position it to lightly blow on the streamers, making them move like a real car wash.

CAUTION! Supervise your toddler during play and never leave the activity set up and unsupervised, as the materials can be an injury hazard.

GROSS MOTOR SKILLS

IMAGINATION

SENSORY DEVELOPMENT

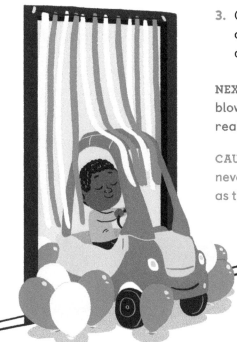

DIY Baby Doll Doctor Kit

It only takes a few minutes to make this pretend doctor kit that your toddler will be using for imaginative play for years to come.

Messiness: **2**
Prep Time: **5 minutes**
Activity Time: **15 minutes**

MATERIALS

Various medical supplies, such as a bulb syringe, medicine dropper, bandages, gauze, cotton balls, craft sticks, stickers, and cotton swabs

Medium plastic bin with lid

Permanent markers in red and black

Baby doll

CAUTION! Monitor your toddler closely when playing with small objects. This activity may not be suitable for children who put objects in their mouths during play.

PREP

1. Place the various supplies inside the bin and secure the lid.

2. Use the red permanent marker to draw a "+" first aid symbol on the lid.

3. Use the black permanent marker to write "Dr. [Child's Name] is in!" below the symbol.

STEPS

1. Give your toddler her new pretend doctor kit. Have her remove the items inside and arrange them on the floor or a table. Discuss each item and brainstorm its possible uses.

2. Flip the empty bin over to use it as an examination table. Prop the lid up nearby to show how it says "Dr. [Child's Name] is in!"

3. Bring a baby doll to the doctor as her first patient. Encourage the doctor to place the baby doll on the examination table and use the various medical supplies to examine and treat the patient.

NEXT LEVEL: Make a pretend thermometer by drawing a red circle at one end of a craft stick, a red line extending from it about halfway up the stick, and black lines with temperature numbers up one side.

Calming Waves Bottle

Make this ocean-themed sensory bottle together and use it to inspire calming thoughts of the ocean. Your toddler's imagination can be its own powerful calming tool!

Messiness: **2**
Prep Time: **None**
Activity Time: **15 minutes**

MATERIALS

1 (12- to 20-ounce) wide-mouth clear plastic drink bottle, empty and clean

Water

Funnel (optional)

Food coloring, blue

Glitter (optional)

Sea-themed decorations, such as small seashells, sand, and small plastic ocean animal toys

Baby oil

Craft glue

STEPS

1. Together with your toddler, fill the bottle about one-third of the way with water, using a funnel if needed. Add 5 to 10 drops of blue food coloring and a few shakes of blue glitter, if using.

2. Ask your toddler to help add seashells, ocean animals, and up to a cup of sand. Help him identify each ocean animal as he adds it to the bottle.

3. Fill the bottle the rest of the way with baby oil.

4. Add some craft glue to the threads on the inner part of the lid and seal it tightly onto the bottle.

5. Show your child how moving and shaking the bottle causes ocean waves and makes the animals and seashells move in the waves. Encourage him to hold and shake the bottle, then watch the contents move as a way to imagine the ocean and feel calm.

NEXT LEVEL: Use seashells and sand from your beach vacation to evoke happy family vacation memories.

CAUTION! Monitor your toddler closely when crafting with small objects. This activity may not be suitable for children who put objects in their mouths during play.

FINE MOTOR SKILLS

IMAGINATION

MINDFULNESS

SOCIAL-EMOTIONAL DEVELOPMENT

VISUAL SPATIAL SKILLS

**GROSS MOTOR
SKILLS**

IMAGINATION

**SENSORY
DEVELOPMENT**

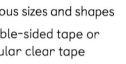

**VISUAL SPATIAL
SKILLS**

Giant Mess-Free Sandcastle

Save up some cardboard boxes and you've got a giant sandcastle activity your toddler will love!

Messiness: **1**
Prep Time: **5 minutes**
Activity Time: **10 minutes**

MATERIALS

Clear packing tape

Cardboard boxes of various sizes and shapes

Double-sided tape or regular clear tape

Cardboard paper towel tubes

Sandpaper (optional)

PREP

1. Use packing tape to tape the boxes shut.

2. Use double-sided tape to cover some of the boxes and/or cardboard paper towel tubes with sandpaper, if using.

STEPS

1. Show the boxes and tubes to your toddler so she can explore and build with them.

2. If using, talk about how sandpaper feels and how it is like sand on the beach.

3. Encourage your toddler to build a giant sand-castle with the boxes and tubes. Help her tape boxes together, as needed.

NEXT LEVEL: Put your toddler into her beachwear! Place a beach towel and beach toys on the floor next to her castle to encourage imaginative beach-themed play.

Magic Counting Wand

Use a little imagination and some sparkly magic to get your toddler creating and then counting.

Messiness: **1**
Prep Time: **5 minutes**
Activity Time: **15 minutes**

MATERIALS

Scissors

Cereal box cardboard or other thin cardboard

Double-sided tape or craft glue

Bamboo skewer

Paint sticks or crayons

Number stickers and self-adhesive sequins (optional)

3 or 4 (1-foot-long) gift wrapping ribbons (optional)

PREP

1. Cut two matching stars out of the cardboard.

2. Use double-sided tape to sandwich them, printed sides together, around the end of the skewer to create a wand. Cut the sharp end off the skewer, if necessary.

STEPS

1. Ask your toddler to color the star on the wand with paint sticks or crayons.

2. Explain that the wand is magic and will help him count things. Encourage him to identify the numbers while adding number stickers, if you have some. Help him add sparkly sequins—more magic!—to the wand.

3. Help your toddler tie some ribbons around the skewer near the star, if you have some.

4. Have him use his new magic counting wand as a pointer while counting specific things around the house or yard.

SIMPLE SWAP: No bamboo skewer? Try using a rigid paper straw or a plastic or wooden ruler.

CAUTION! Monitor your toddler closely when crafting with small objects. This activity may not be suitable for children who put objects in their mouths during play. Be sure to keep your toddler away from sharp scissors.

CREATIVITY

FINE MOTOR SKILLS

IMAGINATION

123
NUMBERS AND COUNTING

FINE MOTOR
SKILLS

IMAGINATION

SENSORY
DEVELOPMENT

Oats and Cereal Farm

Grab some construction paper and clean out the pantry. You've got some farming to do!

Messiness: **3**
Prep Time: **None**
Activity Time: **20 minutes**

MATERIALS

Dried oats

O-shaped cereal

2 small plastic bins

Construction paper in green, yellow, and brown

Large shallow plastic bin

Tape (optional)

Various small farm toys, such as tractors, wagons, and farm animals

STEPS

1. Together with your toddler, pour the oats into one small bin and the O-shaped cereal into the second small bin.

2. Arrange some construction paper on the inside bottom of the large bin to create "farmers' fields." Talk about what each color of paper could be on the farm, such as a field of green grass, a field of brown dirt, or a field of yellow wheat. Help your toddler tape the pieces of paper down, if desired.

3. Help your child gather some small farm toys, such as tractors, wagons, and farm animals, to play with on her farm.

4. Encourage your toddler to use the oats and O-shaped cereal in playing with the farm toys. Suggest she imaginatively scoop and haul all the grains to offer them as animal food or use it as bedding.

AGE ADAPTATION: Allow an older child to use a marker to draw details on the construction paper before play, such as rows of crops, roads, fence lines, and rectangles for barns.

CAUTION! Monitor your toddler closely when playing with small objects.

Penny Grocery Store

Early literacy and math learning abound when your little one goes pretend grocery shopping.

EARLY LITERACY

IMAGINATION

123
NUMBERS AND COUNTING

Messiness: **1**
Prep Time: **None**
Activity Time: **20 minutes**

MATERIALS

Various canned food items

Coffee table or kitchen table

Small blank labels

Marker

Pennies in a change purse

Reusable shopping bag

STEPS

1. Have your toddler help you arrange the canned food items on the table. Help him read the words on them and identify each food item.

2. Ask your toddler to place a label on each food item, then help him write a price, from 1¢ through 10¢, on each label.

3. Give your toddler the change purse full of pennies. Help him count how many pennies he has.

4. Encourage him to go shopping at the pretend grocery store, using the shopping bag to collect various food items.

5. Have him check out by taking each food item out, reading the price on the tag, and counting out the number of pennies needed to pay for each one.

SIMPLE SWAP: Using heavier canned food items for this activity provides extra sensory input for your toddler. If you don't want to use canned food items, however, you could also save up and use empty food boxes from items such as mac and cheese, cereal, snacks, and pasta.

CAUTION! Monitor your toddler closely when playing with small objects. This activity may not be suitable for children who put objects in their mouths during play.

Frog Tongue ABCs

IMAGINATION

ORAL MOTOR
DEVELOPMENT

SENSORY
DEVELOPMENT

▲

SHAPES AND
LETTERS

Ever notice how those party blowers are sort of like tongues? Use the ones left over after a party for this fun frog-themed alphabet activity.

Messiness: **1**
Prep Time: **None**
Activity Time: **15 minutes**

MATERIALS

Party blowers that unravel when blown through

Alphabet magnets, on the refrigerator

STEPS

1. Practice blowing through the party blowers together with your toddler, noticing how they unravel like a frog's tongue. Pretend to be frogs, ribbiting and blowing your party blower tongues.

2. Show your toddler how to blow the party blower toward the letter magnets on the refrigerator to catch letter "flies." Excitedly call out each letter you touch, saying, "I caught an A!"

3. Encourage your toddler to catch a letter fly on the refrigerator, then share in her excitement when she hits one. Help her call out the letter, if needed.

4. Repeat, being sure to ribbit in between each letter she catches!

NEXT LEVEL: Turn it onto a "Find the Letter Fly" game by calling out an "A," and having your toddler find the A magnet, then blow through the party blower to extend her frog tongue and hit the A. Repeat with each letter of the alphabet.

SIMPLE SWAP: If you don't have any party blowers, turn it into a frog hopping game instead. Have your toddler start across the room and hop like a frog to the refrigerator to find the letter you call out. Then have her hop back before you call out the next letter.

Frozen Peas Chef

Toddlers already enjoy pretend cooking. This toddler cooking activity increases the sensory fun with frozen peas!

Messiness: **3**
Prep Time: **5 minutes**
Activity Time: **15 minutes**

MATERIALS

Towels

Large shallow
plastic bin

Various kitchen items,
such as pots, pans,
mixing bowls, serving
spoons, measuring
cups, and dishes (either
toy, old ones, or some
from a thrift store)

Plastic pitcher filled
with water

Frozen peas

PREP

1. Line the floor with the towels and place the large shallow plastic bin on top of them.

2. Add the various kitchen items, including the pitcher of water, to the bin.

3. Add frozen peas to one of the mixing bowls inside the bin.

STEPS

1. Invite your toddler to explore the peas, water, and kitchen items inside the bin.

2. Encourage him to play pretend chef, using the various kitchen items and water to scoop, stir, mix, and cook the peas.

3. Play pretend restaurant and model good manners while requesting and receiving a pretend meal from your little chef.

SIMPLE SWAP: The frozen element of the peas makes for a great sensory experience. But, you could also use any dried beans or macaroni (without water) for pretend cooking play.

CAUTION! The food items used in this activity are not meant to be eaten, so this activity may not be suitable for children who put objects in their mouths during play.

IMAGINATION

SENSORY
DEVELOPMENT

SOCIAL-EMOTIONAL
DEVELOPMENT

VISUAL SPATIAL
SKILLS

FINE MOTOR
SKILLS

IMAGINATION

SENSORY
DEVELOPMENT

VISUAL SPATIAL
SKILLS

Chocolate Dirt Dough Construction Site

Give your child's construction-themed play a scented sensory element with some simple-to-make (and taste-safe) chocolate dirt dough. (Be careful of this activity if you have a dog or cat in your home, as chocolate can be toxic to them.)

Messiness: **4**
Prep Time: **None**
Activity Time: **20 minutes**

MATERIALS

6 cups flour

2 cups cocoa

Large shallow plastic bin

1 cup cooking oil, any kind, plus more as needed

Towels

Toy construction machines and trucks, water-safe

STEPS

1. Have your toddler help you add the flour and cocoa to the bin and stir with your hands to combine.

2. Add in the oil and stir until the mixture forms a light brown dough that sticks together when squeezed. Add in more oil, if needed, until it reaches the desired consistency.

3. Line the floor or surface with towels and place the plastic bin on top. Have your toddler gather her small toy construction machines and trucks to play with inside the bin.

4. Encourage imaginative construction site play, such as pushing dirt, loading dump trucks, making roads, and hauling dirt dough.

NEXT LEVEL: Add some chocolate sandwich cookies for more imaginative construction-themed fun. Encourage hauling cookies and building with them. Crush some up for different-texture dirt and stones.

Toy Store Galore!

Index cards make the perfect pretend money and aisle signs for this toddler-approved toy store activity.

Messiness: 2
Prep Time: None
Activity Time: 20 minutes

MATERIALS

Various toys

10 to 20 index cards

Marker

Small blank labels

Toy shopping cart or reusable shopping bag

IMAGINATION

123
NUMBERS AND COUNTING

SOCIAL-EMOTIONAL DEVELOPMENT

SORTING

VISUAL SPATIAL SKILLS

STEPS

1. Have your toddler gather toys for a pretend toy store while you make around 10 pretend $1 bills using index cards and a marker.

2. Help your toddler sort the toys by type into different sections (or aisles) around the room, such as the building toys and the stuffed animals.

3. Make a simple sign on an index card for each aisle, including an aisle number (from 1 through 5) and type of toy, if desired.

4. Have your toddler add a blank label to each toy, then write a price (from $1 to $5) on each label.

5. Have your toddler count out the pretend dollar bills. Then, invite him to go shopping in the toy store, using a toy shopping cart or shopping bag to collect toys he would like to purchase with his dollar bills.

6. Pretend to be a store associate and ask him if you can help him find something. Give him the aisle number to locate certain toys.

7. When he's done shopping, have him pay by counting out his pretend money. Try switching roles and allow him to be the store associate helping you, the customer.

AGE ADAPTATION: For an older child, create bills in various denominations, such as $1, $5, $10, and $20.

GROSS MOTOR SKILLS

IMAGINATION

VISUAL SPATIAL SKILLS

Outdoor Ride-On Service Station

What's a toddler to do with ride-on toys but with no garage to maintain them? Create an outdoor pretend self-service station, of course!

Messiness: **2**
Prep Time: **5 minutes**
Activity Time: **15 minutes**

MATERIALS

Colored duct tape or colored electrical tape

Recycled plastic squeeze bottles

Water hose

Outdoor ride-on toys

Play tools or kid-friendly real tools, such as wrenches and ratchets

Medium-size cardboard box

PREP

1. Add colored tape around the bottom half of each squeeze bottle to mimic automotive fluids or oil.

2. Make sure the water to the hose is turned off and set up the end of the hose to be used as a pretend gas pump. Position tools and box nearby.

STEPS

1. Invite your child to drive her ride-on toy into the outdoor pretend service station.

2. Help her to prop one end of her ride-on toy up on the cardboard box so she can get underneath the toy and use various tools to fix it.

3. Ask her to use the pretend fluids and oils to refill her car.

4. Have her use the water hose gas pump to gas up her ride-on toy before she heads out of the station.

NEXT LEVEL: If you have sidewalk chalk, draw lines to indicate roads and arrows to indicate the direction cars should pull into the self-service station.

It's a Zoo Around Here!

Gather up all of your child's stuffed animals for some fun and imaginative animal learning.

IMAGINATION

Messiness: 2
Prep Time: None
Activity Time: 20 minutes

MATERIALS

Laundry baskets, large plastic bins, and/or cardboard boxes

Various stuffed animals and/or plastic animal toys

STEPS

1. Have your toddler help place various laundry baskets, bins, and/or boxes on their sides around the room. These are the zoo enclosures.

2. Go on a hunt around the house together for various stuffed animals or animal toys. Use a laundry basket to collect them, if needed.

3. Have your toddler sort the animals by type into the various zoo enclosures. Identify and discuss each animal's characteristics and sounds while doing so. Count the number of animals in each enclosure when you're done.

4. Pretend to be a visitor to the zoo and have your child pretend to be the zoo keeper. Have him give you a tour and tell you about the animals in each zoo enclosure.

AGE ADAPTATION: If you have an older child, have him help make signs for each enclosure, including the animals' name(s) and a drawing to represent the animals.

123
NUMBERS AND COUNTING

ORAL MOTOR DEVELOPMENT

SCIENCE

SOCIAL-EMOTIONAL DEVELOPMENT

SORTING

**GROSS MOTOR
SKILLS**

IMAGINATION

LISTENING

**VISUAL SPATIAL
SKILLS**

Taxi Down the Runway

Your toddler will love this active and imaginative airplane activity, complete with pretend clouds and sky!

Messiness: **2**
Prep Time: **5 minutes**
Activity Time: **15 minutes**

MATERIALS

Painter's tape

Pillows, sheets, and/or blankets, ideally in white and shades of blue

Headphones and safety goggles (optional)

PREP

1. Use painter's tape to make a runway with a dashed center line down the middle of the floor of a hallway or across a room.

2. Place various blue sheets and blankets on the floor and over furniture at the end of the runway. Add white pillows and blankets randomly around the room as pretend clouds.

STEPS

1. Invite your toddler to be a pretend plane by holding her arms out as wings and taxiing (or slowly moving) to her place at the start of the runway.

2. Pretend to be an air traffic controller and wear headphones and safety goggles, if you have them. Use your arms to direct your little airplane into position.

3. Communicate back and forth with your toddler to see when she's ready for takeoff. Signal her to take off down the runway, increasing speed as she goes, and flying off into the sky and clouds. Guide her when she's ready to land back on the runway.

4. Then switch roles and have her play air traffic controller while you fly!

NEXT LEVEL: If you have some extra time, use two cardboard paper towel tubes covered at their ends in red or orange tape to make pretend air traffic control wands.

Baby Bird's Nest

My kids used to love building a giant "nest" in the middle of the living room floor. We would snuggle, read books, or sometimes watch cartoons. Make your own giant nest for some toddler snuggles or imaginative bird-themed play.

Messiness: **2**
Prep Time: **None**
Activity Time: **20 minutes**

MATERIALS

Various cushions, pillows, and blankets

Bird-themed children's books (optional)

STEPS

1. Together with your toddler, place a few couch cushions on the floor, and then use various pillows and blankets to create nest walls in a circle around them.

2. Climb into your nest with your toddler. Snuggle and read some bird-themed children's books, if you have some. Talk about birds and practice bird movements and sounds.

3. Have your toddler curl up into an egg shape. Pretend to be the mama bird keeping your egg warm by snuggling it. Have your little one pretend to crack open his shell and emerge as a baby bird. Pretend to care for your baby bird, eventually encouraging him to hop out of the nest and fly.

NEXT LEVEL: If you have some worm-shaped gummy candies, feed them to your baby bird during your pretend bird play, but only use them if your toddler is capable of chewing them sufficiently without choking.

IMAGINATION

ORAL MOTOR DEVELOPMENT

SCIENCE

SENSORY DEVELOPMENT

Easy Envelope Puppet

CREATIVITY

IMAGINATION

LANGUAGE
DEVELOPMENT

SOCIAL-EMOTIONAL
DEVELOPMENT

Your toddler will love helping you transform a typical envelope into a silly puppet. She'll get beneficial language and social skill practice while playing with it, too.

Messiness: **1**
Prep Time: **5 minutes**
Activity Time: **15 minutes**

MATERIALS

Standard business white envelope (4$\frac{1}{8}$" x 9$\frac{1}{2}$")

Scissors

Washable markers

PREP

1. Seal the envelope flap shut.

2. Fold the envelope in half, flap-side in.

3. Carefully cut along the fold, through only one layer of the envelope. You should be able to now slide your fingers into the cut part on top of the fold and slide your thumb into the cut part on the bottom part of the fold to make a hand puppet.

STEPS

1. Invite your toddler to decorate the puppet with markers.

2. Help her draw lips at the ends of the folded envelope.

3. Help her draw eyes on the top part of the envelope.

4. Use your new puppet friend to tell silly stories, or make multiple puppets and put on a puppet show.

NEXT LEVEL: If you have the time and some basic craft supplies, add a few more creative elements to your envelope puppet. Glue a red paper tongue inside the folded mouth, add googly eyes to the top folded part, or cut fringe hair out of a strip of paper to glue on the top.

CAUTION! Monitor your toddler closely when you are using sharp scissors.

Planting Patterns

Your little one can learn about the science of seeds and plants through this clever pretend play activity. You can easily sneak some pattern learning in, too.

Messiness: **2**
Prep Time: **None**
Activity Time: **15 minutes**

MATERIALS

Pom-poms, in assorted colors, including black or brown

Small plastic food storage containers, one per pom-pom color

Medium-size shallow plastic bin, or baking pan

4 to 6 cardboard paper towel tubes

Scissors (optional)

Plastic watering can or water pitcher

CAUTION! Monitor your toddler closely when you are using sharp scissors and when playing with small objects. This activity may not be suitable for children who put objects in their mouths during play.

STEPS

1. Get your toddler started sorting the pom-poms into separate containers based on color. While he is sorting, line the entire inside bottom of the shallow bin with flattened cardboard paper towel tubes, side-by-side. Use scissors to trim tubes, as needed.

2. Demonstrate how to plant a pretend seed by pressing a small black or brown pom-pom down between two tubes in the bin. Allow your toddler to plant various pom-pom seeds while you explain the way seeds use water and sunlight to grow into plants.

3. Have him use the watering can to pretend to water the seeds he planted.

4. Show him how to grow pretend plants by positioning colorful pom-poms where he planted seeds. Have him grow more plants while you discuss the various flowers or vegetables each one could be.

5. Add some learning by encouraging him to grow plants in simple patterns, such as an **ABA pattern** (red tomato, yellow squash, red tomato . . .) **or an ABBA pattern** (red tomato, yellow squash, yellow squash, red tomato . . .).

NEXT LEVEL: If possible, allow your child to explore real seed packets and plant real seeds instead of just pom-poms.

SKILLS LEARNED

FINE MOTOR SKILLS

IMAGINATION

PATTERNS

SCIENCE

SORTING

CREATIVITY

GROSS MOTOR
SKILLS

IMAGINATION

LISTENING

Musical Dress-Up

This silly spin on traditional musical chairs is perfect for a kids' party or playdate. Plus, it gets the kids dressed up in unique ways to inspire creative storytelling and imaginative play.

Messiness: **1**
Prep Time: **None**
Activity Time: **15 minutes**

MATERIALS

Various dress-up items, such as hats, crowns, scarves, necklaces, vests, sunglasses, and purses

Coffee table or other table

Music

STEPS

1. Have the children help you arrange the various dress-up items around the edges of the coffee table.

2. Explain the rules to the players.

   - When they hear the music, they should dance around the coffee table.
   - When the music stops, they must stop where they are and put on the dress-up item nearest to them.

3. Start the music and encourage creative dancing around the table. Randomly stop the music and watch the children put on their dress-up items. Laugh along while they layer different dress-up items throughout the game.

4. Make up silly names and stories for each dressed-up child at the end of the game.

SIMPLE SWAP: If you don't have a table for the children to dance around, arrange the dress-up items in a circle on the floor. If you only have one child playing, arrange the items along a couch for them to dance back and forth along.

Toddler Engineer

Every time your toddler builds with blocks, she becomes an engineer. Add to the learning and imaginative fun by giving your little engineer a few more everyday materials and a problem to solve.

Messiness: **2**
Prep Time: **5 minutes**
Activity Time: **15 minutes**

MATERIALS

Scissors

1 or more cereal boxes

Toy wagon or laundry basket

8 to 10 canned and boxed food items

4 to 6 toy cars of various sizes

PREP

Cut the front and back off the cereal box (or boxes) to use during play.

STEPS

1. Invite your toddler to bring her wagon along to the pantry to gather various canned and boxed food items. Have her pull the wagon of items back to the play area.

2. Show her the cars and discuss their difference in size. Have her try putting them in order from smallest to largest.

3. Tell her you need an engineer, someone who solves problems by designing and building things, to build an appropriate-size garage for each of your different-size cars. Offer the pieces of cereal box cardboard along with the food items for her to build the garages.

4. Encourage her to problem-solve and test to see if the cars fit in the garages as she builds.

SIMPLE SWAP: Not up for using pantry items? Try this engineering challenge with your toddler's toy building blocks instead. You could still offer additional items to use for building, such as pieces of cardboard, rulers, and plastic party cups.

CAUTION! Be sure to keep your toddler away from sharp scissors.

IMAGINATION

PROBLEM-SOLVING

SCIENCE

VISUAL SPATIAL SKILLS

10

Inexpensive Items for an Imaginative Dress-Up Kit

1. **Winter Items:** You can include things like earmuffs, scarves, and mittens.

2. **Hats:** Try to find a range of hats, such as ball caps, cowboy hats, and bonnets.

3. **Old Costume Jewelry:** Check thrift stores and yard sales for sparkly, chunky pieces.

4. **Beach Items:** Add things like sunglasses, goggles, and flippers.

5. **Empty Makeup Compacts:** Clean them out and use nail polish to add pretend makeup color inside them.

6. **Halloween Costumes:** Save old costumes from previous years or buy some on clearance.

7. **Crowns and Tiaras:** Grab some from the dollar store or make them out of pipe cleaners.

8. **Purses and Handbags:** Check thrift stores and yard sales for bags of different colors and sizes.

9. **Face Paint:** Grab some on sale after Halloween.

10. **Leftover Party Supplies:** Get more use out of leftover party hats and blowers.

* 6 *
Outdoor Adventure

In today's technology-soaked world, it's more important than ever to get our kids outside. Tech activity isn't always bad. Technology has allowed my kids to play educational games, research unique hobbies, and connect with long-distance family members. However, a child's technology use needs to be balanced with a healthy dose of non-tech play and learning. The good news is that toddlerhood is full of curiosity and natural wonder, making it the perfect time to foster a love of nature and being outdoors.

Being outside generally facilitates active and messy play, which aids in gross motor skill development and benefits the sensory system. Speaking of sensory, nature is brimming with textures, scents, sounds, and spectacle. Your toddler may smell the scent of wildflowers, feel cool grass on their bare feet, or hear birds chirping in the trees. Not only will they love these new sensations, but they can also learn a lot by experiencing them. So, let's go outside!

SKILLS LEARNED

FINE MOTOR SKILLS

PROBLEM-SOLVING

SCIENCE

SENSORY DEVELOPMENT

VISUAL SPATIAL SKILLS

Sandbox Tubes and Funnel Fun

Sandbox play is a staple of childhood—at least it was for my kids! Sand already offers great sensory opportunities. Add in a few everyday household items, and your little one will be exploring simple physics concepts, too!

Messiness: **4**
Prep Time: **None**
Activity Time: **20 minutes**

MATERIALS

3 (or more) cardboard paper towel tubes of various sizes

1 (or more) funnel(s)

3 (or more) plastic food storage containers of various shapes and sizes

Small toy cars and trucks (optional)

Sandbox

STEPS

1. Give your toddler the cardboard paper towel tubes, funnel(s), plastic bins, and toy cars and trucks to play with in the sandbox. Allow him time for open-ended play and experimentation with the objects.

2. Encourage him to prop tubes up on containers at varying angles and experiment with running toy cars and trucks through them.

3. Discuss ramps and how the different angles and different amounts of force (pushing of the car into the tube ramp) affect the speed of the car.

4. Discuss tunnels and where you might see them in real life, such as under a bridge or in the subway.

NEXT LEVEL: Check your garage or the local hardware store for different-length pieces of PVC pipe to use instead of the cardboard paper towel tubes. Then, you can experiment with running water through the funnels and pipes during play.

Kiddie Pool Squirt Race

Gather your toddler's siblings or grab some neighbor friends for this fun kiddie pool game that can be played while the kids are inside the pool or out!

Messiness: **4**
Prep Time: **5 minutes**
Activity Time: **10 minutes**

MATERIALS

Kiddie pool

Water

Squeeze bottles or squirt toys, one per racer

Rubber ducks, one per racer

SKILLS LEARNED

FINE MOTOR SKILLS

SCIENCE

SENSORY DEVELOPMENT

VISUAL SPATIAL SKILLS

PREP

Fill the kiddie pool with water. Then, fill each squeeze bottle or squirt toy with water.

STEPS

1. Demonstrate how to squirt at a duck in the water to make it move. Discuss how the force of the water hitting the duck made it move.

2. Explain the rules of the game.

   - On the count of three, each racer should place their duck in the water in front of them and use their squeeze bottle to squirt water at their duck, making it move across the water to the other side of the pool.
   - The first duck to touch the other side wins.

3. With all of the racers at one edge of the pool (either inside or kneeling outside of it), count to three and watch the squirt race fun! Cheer on each duck as it makes it to the other side.

SIMPLE SWAP: No rubber ducks? Any toy boats, floating bathtub toys, or plastic ball pit balls should also work.

CAUTION! Always supervise your toddler closely around water.

LANGUAGE
DEVELOPMENT

SCIENCE

SENSORY
DEVELOPMENT

VISUAL SPATIAL
SKILLS

Puddle Splash Experiment

Embrace your little one's innate attraction to mud puddles by using one for a hands-on science experiment.

Messiness: **5**
Prep Time: **None**
Activity Time: **15 minutes**

MATERIALS

Mud puddle

Various water-friendly outdoor toys

Various nature objects, such as stones, pinecones, acorns, and small sticks

Toy wagon or laundry basket

Hose with water (optional)

STEPS

1. Together with your toddler, locate a mud puddle!

2. Gather various water-friendly outdoor toys and nature objects. Have your toddler pull a toy wagon around to collect them, if possible. Or, collect them in a laundry basket. Bring them to the mud puddle.

3. Have your toddler choose one item she collected, identify it, then drop it into the mud puddle and observe the splash. Remove the item from the mud puddle and set it aside.

4. Have her choose and identify another item. Talk about how this item compares to the first item, using words such as *smaller, bigger, lighter,* and *heavier.* Then, have her drop the item into the puddle and observe the splash. Discuss whether this splash was bigger than the first.

5. Repeat until all objects have been dropped in the mud puddle and discussed. Hose off your toddler, if needed!

AGE ADAPTATION: For a more advanced child, add to the learning by explaining gravity as the force that makes everything fall down to the ground. Challenge her to drop two different-size items into the puddle, from the same height and at the same time, to see which hits first. Discuss how the items go the same speed and hit at the same time, regardless of weight or size.

Bubble Pop Challenge

As far as I'm concerned, bubbles are a toddlerhood must! Blowing bubbles helped me avert more than one toddler tantrum over the years. You can obviously blow bubbles inside, but their soapiness makes them ideal for outside play. Here's a fun way to turn your outdoor bubble fun into an educational game your toddler will love.

SKILLS LEARNED

123
NUMBERS AND COUNTING

SENSORY DEVELOPMENT

VISUAL SPATIAL SKILLS

Messiness: **2**
Prep Time: **None**
Activity Time: **10 minutes**

MATERIALS

Bubbles and a bubble wand

STEPS

1. Tell your child you have a challenge for him: to count and pop as many bubbles as he can each time you blow some.

2. Tell him to get his pointer finger ready, then blow some bubbles. Help him count each time he pops a bubble. Celebrate the total number of bubbles your toddler pops.

3. Repeat and see if he can pop a higher number of bubbles each time. Or, try taking turns to see who can pop the most.

SIMPLE SWAP: If you're all out of bubbles, try making your own. Simply stir together 2 cups of warm water, 1 cup of dish soap, and about 4 teaspoons of sugar. Then, make a bubble wand with a pipe cleaner.

Outdoor Spiral Art

CREATIVITY

MINDFULNESS

PATTERNS

SENSORY
DEVELOPMENT

SOCIAL-EMOTIONAL
DEVELOPMENT

Take the art-making outside with this activity that's packed with creativity, sensory input, early math practice, and even social-emotional learning!

Messiness: **3**
Prep Time: **5 minutes**
Activity Time: **15 minutes**

MATERIALS

Various nature objects, such as pebbles, acorns, leaves, dandelions, and small pinecones

Various food items, such as dry pasta, corn kernels, and dry beans (optional)

Medium-size shallow plastic bin

Sidewalk chalk

PREP

1. Gather the various nature objects and food items inside the bin and place the bin on the sidewalk.

2. Draw a three- to four-foot-wide spiral on the sidewalk using sidewalk chalk.

STEPS

1. Invite your toddler to place pebbles along the chalk-drawn spiral line. While doing so, explain how looking at, touching, or walking along a spiral sometimes helps people feel calm.

2. Encourage her to fill the spaces between the stone spiral lines with other objects.

3. Add some learning by helping her make simple patterns with the objects, such as an ABA pattern (leaf, pebble, leaf . . .) or an ABBA pattern (leaf, pebble, pebble, leaf . . .) along the spiral.

4. When she is done creating her spiral art, encourage her to sit quietly while looking at her art and following the spiral with her eyes. Talk with her about how she feels before and after.

NEXT LEVEL: If possible, take a picture of your toddler's completed spiral art from above. Then, have it printed and use the photo as a tool next time she needs to calm down. Teach your toddler how to move her finger slowly over the spiral in the photo when she needs to calm her body or emotions.

Yummy Chocolate Mud Pie

Toddlers are typically pretty messy in the kitchen. Take the messy food fun outside with this toddler-friendly and delicious mud pie recipe!

Messiness: **3**
Prep Time: **None**
Activity Time: **20 minutes**

MATERIALS

Picnic table or other flat surface

Kid-friendly plate utensils

1 snack-size chocolate pudding cup

1 mini ready-to-eat graham cracker piecrust

3 jelly worm candies

2 chocolate sandwich cookies

STEPS

1. Invite your toddler to the picnic table (or another flat surface) to make a mud pie. Explain that it will not actually be made of mud, but instead it will be made of yummy ingredients that just look like mud.

2. Ask him to use a spoon to transfer the pudding from the snack cup into the mini piecrust.

3. Give him the worm candies to add to the top of the pudding.

4. Have him crush the cookies with his hands over the top of the pie and worms.

5. Enjoy his chocolate mud pie snack!

NEXT LEVEL: If you have a playdate or kids' party, you could make a large chocolate mud pie using chocolate pudding and worm candies in a full-size graham cracker piecrust. Seal a bunch of chocolate sandwich cookies inside a gallon-size plastic zip-top bag, and let the kids take turns pounding on the bag to crush the cookies and then sprinkle the crumbs on the pie.

CAUTION! Only use the gummy worm candies if you know your child can sufficiently chew them. Always supervise closely while your child is eating.

Nature Hunt Weaving

A plain old paper plate and some rubber bands make a clever tool for collecting nature objects. Your toddler will be thrilled to keep her findings, and she'll be getting some great fine motor skills practice, too.

Messiness: **2**
Prep Time: **5 minutes**
Activity Time: **15 minutes**

MATERIALS

Scissors

Sturdy paper plate

5 to 8 rubber bands

Various natural materials, such as grass, wildflowers, leaves, dandelions, and small twigs

PREP

1. Use the scissors to cut half-inch snips every inch or so around two opposite sides of the paper plate.

2. Stretch a rubber band around the plate and position it inside a snip on one side of the plate and the corresponding snip on the other side, creating something that looks like woven rubber bands, and which will hold the nature objects in place.

3. Repeat, adding more rubber bands, parallel to the first, across the entire plate.

STEPS

1. Demonstrate for your toddler how to slightly lift a rubber band to weave an object from nature, such as a leaf, under it.

2. Have her find a nature object nearby and practice with it.

3. Invite her on a nature hunt to find more nature objects and weave them under different rubber bands on the plate. Talk about the objects as she finds them.

AGE ADAPTATION: A younger toddler will likely only weave a natural material under one rubber band. However, an older child could be taught how to weave materials under one rubber band, then over the next one, then under the next one, and so on. An older child could also help position the rubber bands on the plate during prep.

CAUTION! Always keep your toddler away from sharp scissors.

Mud-Paint Alphabet

Give your toddler a taste of ancient times by mixing up your very own paint using mud!

FINE MOTOR
SKILLS

SCIENCE

SHAPES AND
LETTERS

VISUAL SPATIAL
SKILLS

Messiness: **4**
Prep Time: **None**
Activity Time: **20 minutes**

MATERIALS

Dirt

Medium-size plastic bin or plastic mixing bowl

Large paintbrush

Water

Sidewalk chalk

STEPS

1. Add some dirt to the bin, and have your toddler help stir it with a paintbrush while you add a little bit of water at a time until it reaches a paint-like consistency. Discuss how, many years ago, ancient people made paint this way to create cave paintings and decorate their clothing.

2. Use a piece of sidewalk chalk to write the letter A on the pavement. Have your toddler trace over it with his finger, and then try painting over it with the paintbrush and mud paint.

3. Write the letter B next to the letter A and have him do the same thing, tracing and then painting the letter. Repeat for each letter of the alphabet.

AGE ADAPTATION: Personalize the learning fun to your child's level by replacing the alphabet with numbers, basic shapes, or even sight words. You could also make it a game by writing letters or numbers randomly on the sidewalk and calling them out, one at a time, for him to find and paint.

Magic Mix-and-Pour Colors

Scooping, mixing, and pouring can be challenging for toddlers, yet they love practicing these grown-up skills. Practice outside, where spills won't matter, and incorporate the science of color mixing to make this toddler activity even more educational and fun!

COLORS

FINE MOTOR SKILLS

SCIENCE

VISUAL SPATIAL SKILLS

Messiness: **4**
Prep Time: **5 minutes**
Activity Time: **10 minutes**

MATERIALS

6 small clear plastic food storage containers

Picnic table or other flat surface

Food coloring in red, yellow, and blue

Plastic pitcher of water

Measuring cups

PREP

1. Position three of the plastic containers in a row on a picnic table or another flat surface. Add a few drops of red food coloring to one container, a few drops of yellow to the second container, and a few drops of blue to the third.

2. Place the pitcher of water, remaining containers, and measuring cups nearby.

STEPS

1. Invite your child to practice her pouring skills by pouring water from the pitcher into each of the containers containing only food coloring. Help her identify each color as the water hits the food coloring and changes color.

2. Encourage her to use the measuring cups as scoops to experiment with transferring the different-colored water into the empty containers.

3. Share in her excitement when she discovers how mixing two colors of water makes a new color. Challenge her to identify any new colors created.

SIMPLE SWAP: If you don't have any food coloring in the kitchen, you could use a small amount of washable paint instead. Just keep a spoon nearby for mixing the paint and water after pouring.

EARLY LITERACY

IMAGINATION

**LANGUAGE
DEVELOPMENT**

Instant Outdoor Story Time Tent

Who says story time has to be inside? Make a simple story time tent outside to encourage your toddler's love of books, no matter where he is.

Messiness: **3**
Prep Time: **5 minutes**
Activity Time: **15 minutes**

MATERIALS

2 or more outdoor chairs

1 or 2 old sheets

4 or more beach towel clips, large binder clips, or utility clips

Children's books

Small basket or bin

Hand wipes (optional)

PREP

Position two or more outdoor chairs about four to six feet apart. Drape one or more sheets across the backs of the chairs to create a tent underneath. Use clips to secure the sheets onto the chairs.

STEPS

1. Have your toddler join you inside the house to gather some children's books in a basket. Consider choosing books with nature or animal themes.

2. Take the basket of books to the tent and invite your toddler inside the tent for story time. If possible, have hand wipes ready to clean dirty fingers before touching the books.

3. Allow free time for reading and exploring the various books.

NEXT LEVEL: Add imagination and fun by pretending the tent is an outdoor library. Hold a story time, and then have your toddler choose books to borrow. Pretend to scan the book at checkout. Take turns being the librarian.

CAUTION! Never leave the play materials set up when not supervising your toddler, as they can be an injury hazard.

COLORS

GROSS MOTOR
SKILLS

SCIENCE

SENSORY
DEVELOPMENT

VISUAL SPATIAL
SKILLS

Color-of-the-Day Kiddie Swim

My kids loved choosing a color of the day when they were young. Throughout the day, we would eat foods of that color, scribble pictures in that color, and spy the color everywhere. Have some color-themed fun with your toddler by setting up a color-of-the-day swim outside!

Messiness: **4**
Prep Time: **5 minutes**
Activity Time: **15 minutes**

MATERIALS

Kiddie pool

Water

Water-friendly toys, all the same color, such as plastic cars or trucks, bath toys, plastic ball pit balls, and beach toys

Small plastic laundry basket or large plastic bin

PREP

Fill the kiddie pool with water.

STEPS

1. Ask your toddler to choose a color and go on a hunt around the house for water-friendly toys in that color.

2. Place the ones you find in a plastic laundry basket. Encourage lots of color recognition of toys and talk about which toys are water-safe (such as plastic toys) while hunting.

3. Take the basket of toys out to the kiddie pool, and have your child transfer them into the pool. Encourage him to notice which toys sink and which ones float.

4. Help your child into the pool for some open-ended water play with the color-themed toys.

NEXT LEVEL: If you have color bath tablets, add one in the matching color to the pool water and swish it around to help it dissolve. Share in your toddler's excitement over the water turning color!

CAUTION! Always supervise your toddler closely around water.

Toddler-Size Number Bowling

Kids' bowling games are always smart to play outside, because then there's no worry over balls and pins breaking something. The extra space outdoors also allows you to supersize the pins so your toddler can actually *be* the bowling ball!

GROSS MOTOR SKILLS

123

NUMBERS AND COUNTING

VISUAL SPATIAL SKILLS

Messiness: **2**
Prep Time: **5 minutes**
Activity Time: **15 minutes**

MATERIALS

Tape

6 to 10 medium cardboard boxes

Marker

PREP

Tape the boxes shut. With the boxes positioned vertically, write a different number (beginning with 1) on one side of each box.

STEPS

1. Position the numbered boxes vertically, in a triangle pattern, like bowling pins when set up.

2. Invite your toddler to be the bowling ball! Tell her to run toward the boxes, knock into them, and try to tip them over.

3. Have her count how many boxes she knocked down. Help her identify the numbers on the boxes as you set them back up so she can bowl again.

4. Repeat, allowing her to bowl and count for as long as she is interested in doing so.

SIMPLE SWAP: The cardboard boxes could be replaced with empty and cleaned 2-liter plastic soda bottles or milk cartons. And, you could also allow your toddler to bowl into them with a ride-on toy or by more traditional means, such as rolling a rubber ball at them!

123

NUMBERS AND
COUNTING

SENSORY
DEVELOPMENT

VISUAL SPATIAL
SKILLS

Sandbox Phone Number Puzzle

Not every toddler will be able to memorize a caregiver's phone number, but, for safety reasons, the earlier a child knows it, the better. This activity exposes your toddler to your phone number in a fun and low-pressure way—by playing in his sandbox!

Messiness: **4**
Prep Time: **None**
Activity Time: **10 minutes**

MATERIALS

Sandbox

Foam bath numbers, plastic number magnets, or plastic number-shape puzzle pieces

Spray bottle with water (optional)

STEPS

1. Review your phone number with your toddler while you make an impression of it in the sand with foam numbers. (If the sand doesn't hold an impression, try misting it with water first.)

2. Have him look away while you randomly arrange the foam numbers near the impression.

3. Invite him to do the phone number puzzle by placing each foam number inside its matching number impression. Encourage number identification and phone number practice while doing so.

AGE ADAPTATION: If your toddler isn't ready for phone number learning yet, simply use numbers 1 through 5 or 1 through 10 for the sandbox puzzle instead. Older children could also use foam bath letters or letter magnets to make name or sight words puzzles.

Less Messy Outdoor Bakery

Not up for making messy mud pies? Use your old kitchen items for an instant outdoor bakery using dried split peas, dried beans, and playdough instead of messy mud.

FINE MOTOR SKILLS

IMAGINATION

PATTERNS

SENSORY DEVELOPMENT

Messiness: **4**
Prep Time: **5 minutes**
Activity Time: **15 minutes**

MATERIALS

Various kitchen items, such as pie pans, mixing bowls, rolling pin, cookie cutters, measuring cups, and utensils

Playdough, store-bought or using recipe on page 44

Dried split peas and dried beans

PREP

Arrange a variety of mixing bowls, pie pans, and other kitchen items as well as playdough on a flat surface outside. Add some dried split peas and dried beans to some of the mixing bowls.

STEPS

1. Invite your toddler to play with her new outdoor kitchen. Allow free time for her to explore and experiment with the various tools and materials.

2. Help her use the rolling pin to flatten the playdough and line the inside of a pie pan with it to make a pretend piecrust. Have her add the peas or beans for the pie filling. Help her make a pretend pie top crust using strips or long rolls of playdough.

3. Encourage her to make pretend cookies by cutting them out of flattened playdough with cookie cutters. Show her how to press peas and beans into the playdough cookies for decoration. Add some simple pattern learning by having her arrange them in an ABA pattern (bean, pea, bean . . .) or an ABBA pattern (bean, pea, pea, bean . . .).

NEXT LEVEL: If you have some old plastic plates and utensils, use them to extend the imaginative play and have your child serve you baked goods in her pretend bakery. Practice good manners and listening skills by ordering baked goods.

COLORS

CREATIVITY

FINE MOTOR
SKILLS

SENSORY
DEVELOPMENT

Nature Sandwich Printmaking

Let your little one hunt for and examine nature objects while getting creative with paint, color, and printmaking!

Messiness: **4**
Prep Time: **None**
Activity Time: **20 minutes**

MATERIALS

Various flat nature objects, such as leaves, small twigs, flat stones, flowers, and blades of grass

Small plastic bin (optional)

Washable paint

Paintbrush

White paper

Container of water

STEPS

1. Go on a hunt around the yard with your toddler looking for various flat nature objects. Use a plastic bin to gather them, if possible.

2. Place the nature objects on a flat washable surface. Have your child choose a nature object, paint it one color, and then place it paint-side down on a piece of white paper.

3. Have him repeat, painting various nature objects and placing them paint-side down on the same paper. Encourage color identification and discuss each nature object while doing so.

4. Help him position another piece of paper over the first, sandwiching the painted nature objects between the two, and press down all over it.

5. Remove the top paper and the objects to see the nature prints they left on the bottom paper. Set it aside to dry. Repeat to make more colorful nature prints.

SIMPLE SWAP: If you're not up for painting, you could sandwich the nature objects between the two sheets of paper and rub over the top with the side of a crayon to create nature crayon rubbings. Or, you could try pressing the objects into flattened playdough to make nature impressions.

Go Alphabet Fish!

Turn your kiddie pool into a fish pond—full of alphabet fish! Your toddler will have fun playing an active game of Go Fish! while practicing her motor skills and letter recognition at the same time.

Messiness: **3**
Prep Time: **5 minutes**
Activity Time: **15 minutes**

MATERIALS

Kiddie pool

Water

Foam bath letters, plastic letter magnets, or water-friendly letter puzzle pieces

Mesh strainer

SKILLS LEARNED

FINE MOTOR SKILLS

SHAPES AND LETTERS

VISUAL SPATIAL SKILLS

PREP

Fill the pool with water and add the foam letters to the pool.

STEPS

1. Invite your toddler to kneel or stand at the edge of the pool to play a game of Go Fish!

2. Explain the rules:

   - You will call out letters of the alphabet one at a time (either randomly or in alphabetical order).
   - She needs to use her strainer to fish each letter out of the water after you call it out.

3. After she has caught all of the letters, help her put them in alphabetical order. Then, sing the alphabet song together.

SIMPLE SWAP: No kiddie pool? You could also play this game with a large plastic bin filled with water or even use your bathtub. You could also substitute a large slotted serving spoon or small fish net for the strainer.

CAUTION! Always supervise your toddler closely around water.

FINE MOTOR
SKILLS

SCIENCE

VISUAL SPATIAL
SKILLS

"Disappearing Me" Painting

Painting with water outside on a sidewalk or fence is an easy activity most toddlers enjoy. Make it even more fun by tracing your toddler on the sidewalk and watching his reaction when his water-painted self disappears!

Messiness: **3**
Prep Time: **None**
Activity Time: **15 minutes**

MATERIALS

Sidewalk chalk

Container of water

Large paintbrush

STEPS

1. Have your child lay down on the sidewalk or pavement, positioning his arms and legs any way he wants. Trace around his entire body with a piece of sidewalk chalk, then have him get up.

2. Have him use a paintbrush and water to "paint" inside the outline of himself.

3. While he paints, discuss the way the water makes the sidewalk darken, because it absorbs some of the water. Then, discuss how the water starts to disappear, because the warm air and sunshine make it evaporate into the air and up into the clouds.

NEXT LEVEL: Add some creativity by inviting your little one to draw details or patterns inside of his body tracing using sidewalk chalk before he begins painting.

Digging for Silver Treasure

Take sandbox play to another level with one everyday kitchen item and an imaginative treasure hunt theme!

Messiness: **4**
Prep Time: **5 minutes**
Activity Time: **15 minutes**

MATERIALS

Aluminum foil

Sandbox

Sand toy shovel and/or rake (optional)

PREP

Create five or more crumpled-up pieces of aluminum foil in various sizes. Bury the pieces of silver treasure in the sandbox, ideally when your toddler isn't looking.

STEPS

1. Invite your toddler to dig for treasure in her sandbox. Allow her to use sand toys, if desired.

2. Celebrate with her when she discovers a silver treasure. Have her set it aside and continue digging for more treasure.

3. Each time she finds a piece of treasure, help your toddler count the total number of pieces she has found.

4. Repeat, until all pieces of treasure are found.

NEXT LEVEL: Add some more fine motor skills practice, more early math learning, and an element of surprise by wrapping a coin inside each piece of aluminum foil before burying them. Have your toddler unwrap the foil to get the coins out. Help her identify the coins and sort them.

SKILLS LEARNED

FINE MOTOR SKILLS

123

NUMBERS AND COUNTING

SENSORY DEVELOPMENT

VISUAL SPATIAL SKILLS

FINE MOTOR
SKILLS

SCIENCE

SENSORY
DEVELOPMENT

VISUAL SPATIAL
SKILLS

Outdoor Observer Telescope

Make a simple pretend telescope with your little one to inspire lots of careful observation of nature and maybe an I Spy game or two.

Messiness: 2
Prep Time: None
Activity Time: 15 minutes

MATERIALS

Cardboard paper towel tube

Stickers, ideally nature- or animal-themed

Washable markers (optional)

STEPS

1. Invite your toddler to decorate the outside of the cardboard paper towel tube with stickers and markers. Discuss how it will become a telescope to help him see things in nature.

2. Demonstrate how to hold the telescope up to one eye and look through it to see something across the yard. Invite him to try it.

3. Play a simple game of I Spy by calling out a nature object or animal for him to find by looking through his telescope. Then have him call out something for you to find. Repeat, taking turns finding various nature objects or animals. Talk about the characteristics of each object or animal as you do so.

NEXT LEVEL: If you don't have a paper towel tube but have a couple of cardboard toilet paper tubes, tape or glue two of them together to create binoculars for your toddler to decorate and use instead.

Sun Launch Game

This simple spin on a kids' parachute game can be played with one toddler or with a group. It's super fun and great for strengthening motor skills, too.

Messiness: 2
Prep Time: None
Activity Time: 10 minutes

MATERIALS

Toddler bedsheet
or large beach towel

Inflated balloon or
a lightweight toy ball,
ideally yellow

SKILLS
LEARNED

GROSS MOTOR
SKILLS

SENSORY
DEVELOPMENT

VISUAL SPATIAL
SKILLS

STEPS

1. Have your toddler hold each corner of the short end of the sheet while you hold the two corners at the other short end. Stand a few feet apart so the sheet is spread out between you.

2. Place the balloon on the sheet and explain that the sun (the balloon) fell out of the sky and needs help getting back up into it!

3. Practice moving the sheet up and down a few times with your toddler before lifting it as fast as you can to launch the balloon up as high as you can. Celebrate as you watch how high it goes.

4. Repeat, as often as your toddler has interest, and see if you can launch it higher into the sky each time.

NEXT LEVEL: If you have more players, have them stand and hold the sheet about equal distances around the edges and work together to launch the balloon into the sky. Use a larger sheet or light-weight blanket for larger groups. Or, separate the kids into two groups, each with their own smaller sheet or beach towel, and try tossing a lightweight ball back and forth between the two.

10

Ways to Play Outside in Rainy or Snowy Weather

1. **Wet Sidewalk Chalk Art:** Use sidewalk chalk on the wet sidewalk to create vibrant, temporary art.

2. **Snow Name Shuffle:** Shuffle your feet as you walk to spell out your child's name in the snow. Show them how to do the same thing to make their own letters.

3. **Raindrop Meditation:** Practice mindfulness, meditation, and listening while raindrops patter on your umbrellas.

4. **Snow Spray Art:** Use food coloring to color water, pour the water into spray bottles, and then spray the snow to make colorful snowy art.

5. **Snow Maze:** Shovel a maze or winding path in the snow to walk through.

6. **Crawly Count:** Hunt for and count snails or worms on a rainy day.

7. **Painted Snowman:** Make a snowman and paint details on it with watercolor paints.

8. **Rainy Day Watercolors:** Paint the sidewalk with watercolor in the rain and watch what the raindrops do to it.

9. **Snow Kitchen:** Use old kitchen supplies for pretend snow kitchen play.

10. **Puddle Boat Play:** Take small plastic bins outside to use as boats in rain puddles.

Resources & References

ACTIVITY PRINTABLES

You can find printable resources at www.B-InspiredMama.com/tag/printables.

CHILDREN'S BOOKS

Goodnight, Goodnight, Construction Site by Sherri Duskey Rinker and
Tom Lichtenheld

   This book was one of my construction-machine-loving Sawyer's favorites.
It pairs perfectly with Chocolate Dirt Dough Construction Site (page 106).

The Wide-Mouthed Frog (A Pop-Up Book) by Keith Faulkner and
Jonathan Lambert

   The wide-mouthed frog in this silly book and all of his wide-mouthed friends
will surely get your little one giggling. Read this one before you do Frog Tongue
ABCs (page 104).

Mouse Paint by Ellen Stoll Walsh

   This cute book about three mice who accidentally mix colors has been my
go-to book for teaching little ones basic color theory for years. Read it with
activities that teach color-mixing, like Coffee Filter Color-Mixing (page 51) and
Magic Mix-and-Pour Colors (page 129).

1, 2, 3 to the Zoo: A Counting Book by Eric Carle

   I have adored Eric Carle books since I visited the Eric Carle Museum of
Picture Book Art for research in graduate school. His painted collage illustration
style is perfect for toddlers. Read this one when you do the zoo-themed activity
It's a Zoo Around Here! (page 109).

OTHER ACTIVITY BOOKS

The Outdoor Toddler Activity Book: 100+ Fun Learning Activities for Outside Play by Krissy Bonning-Gould

My very first toddler activity book! This book has lots of fun and educational toddler activities for outside play that you can do no matter the weather or season.

The Rainy Day Toddler Activity Book: 100+ Fun Learning Activities for Indoor Play by Krissy Bonning-Gould

The companion to the outdoor toddler activity book, also written by me! This book offers tons of fun and educational toddler activities for indoor play.

Play & Learn Toddler Activities Book: 200+ Fun Activities for Early Learning by Angela Thayer

Here's another helpful book you'll want to have handy through the toddler years. Written by my blogging-mama friend, Angela Thayer (founder of Teaching Mama), *Play & Learn Toddler Activities Book* is the forerunner that inspired this book and its outdoor activities predecessor. As a former teacher and fellow mama of three, she has tons of experience and expertise in child development, hands-on learning, and, of course, play!

Activities for 1 Year Olds: Fun Doable Ideas for Your Toddler by Nicolette Roux and Heather Knapp

This book is full of simple yet captivating ideas for the littlest of toddlers, written by my longtime blogging friends, Nicolette and Heather.

Awesome Science Experiments for Kids: 100+ Fun STEM/STEAM Projects and Why They Work by Crystal Chatterton

Science experiments are fascinating for kids of all ages! Grab this book for simple science activities your toddler will love.

First Art for Toddlers and Twos: Open-Ended Art Experiences by MaryAnn F. Kohl

My former-art-teacher heart loves everything MaryAnn Kohl writes. This book, in particular, focuses on inspiring little ones to experience and learn through art-making activities. Process over product, always!

My Toddler Talks: Strategies and Activities to Promote Your Child's Language Development by Kimberly Scanlon

This book is full of valuable information and activity ideas, from a licensed speech-language pathologist, for any parent who wants to support their toddler's language development.

WEBSITES AND BLOGS

My Bored Toddler: MyBoredToddler.com

This blog is a go-to resource for creative and educational ideas, specifically for little ones. Plus, the ideas shared on this site are usually inexpensive and doable by anyone.

Fun with Mama: FunWithMama.com

My blogging friend, Nadia, has developed an extensive resource of fun kids' activities, early learning printables, and helpful family lifestyle resources on her blog throughout the years.

Toddler Approved: ToddlerApproved.com

Kristina has been sharing fun and creative activities for little ones for years! She aims for each activity to foster creativity and a love for learning.

Growing a Jeweled Rose: GrowingAJeweledRose.com

Crystal has worked for years to make this blog an extensive resource for fun kids' play ideas. Check out her collection of play recipes for your toddler!

Teaching 2 and 3 Year Olds: Teaching2and3YearOlds.com

Sheryl Cooper is an experienced toddler and preschool teacher who shares all of her tried-and-tested early learning ideas on her blog. But her ideas aren't just for the classroom; they're simple enough for any busy mom to pull off, too.

Red Ted Art: RedTedArt.com

Red Ted Art is loaded with clever and creative craft ideas for kids of all ages. Maggie, my longtime blogging friend and the creative genius behind the blog, has also written a *Red Ted Art* craft book and has an extensive following on her *Red Ted Art* YouTube channel.

Teaching Mama: TeachingMama.org

Angela Thayer uses her years of teaching experience to develop fun learning activities that toddlers and preschoolers love. Plus, as mentioned, she authored the popular toddler activity book, *Play & Learn Toddler Activities Book: 200+ Fun Activities for Early Learning.*

REFERENCE

"Serve and Return." Center on the Developing Child. Harvard University. Accessed March 6, 2019. DevelopingChild.Harvard.edu/science/key-concepts/serve-and-return.

Index

Acknowledgments

I find myself speechless as I begin to write my third set of acknowledgments in just six short months. I feel honored for this opportunity to share fun and creativity with little ones and their caregivers.

Thank you, first, to the mamas, fathers, caregivers, and teachers who have supported and spread the love of B-InspiredMama over the past 10 years. You did so because of your love for the children in your life, which is commendable and appreciated.

Thank you, also, to Callisto Media for seeing potential in me and B-Inspired Mama and providing me with this platform to reach even more little ones.

I so often focus on moms in my writing because, obviously, they are who I relate to most, but the incredible dads in my life deserve special recognition as well. My former husband, Brian Bonning, has remained a support for me and an amazing dad for our Sawyer and Priscilla throughout the entirety of my creative B-Inspired Mama journey. My husband, Clifford Gould II, jumped in without hesitation as a devoted stepfather of those two, is favorite-person-in-the-world of our J.C., and the ultimate cheerleader of me and everything I do. My brother, Josh Sherman, always finds time to love on my kids and support me amid his own crazy journey parenting three awesome kids. And, finally, my father, Raymond Sherman, has shown me the value of hard work and dedication, taking risks and following dreams, and most importantly, loving your family and others. Thank you, Dad.

But I cannot leave out my mama, Tammy Sherman. I'm so thankful to have you as my mother, as my best friend, and as Mimi to my babies.

I am so grateful for my life full of friends and support people, too. Thank you, Aunt Kelly, for your words of wisdom and prayers over the years. Thank you, Jenny Barrett, for always proving the power of friendship regardless of time between visits. And, thank you, Kelly Cummings, for always accepting me in all my mess.

Of course, as I've stated in previous books, my three children are the true authors of these books, as they are the authors of my mama heart and inspire every breath and idea. Sawyer, Priscilla, and J.C., it is my favorite hobby to watch you grow as the amazing humans you are. Thank you for your love and patience while I have stretched my own creativity and grown a little while writing these books. You are my world-changers.

About the Author

Krissy Bonning-Gould is a former art teacher with a master's degree in K–12 art education turned full-time blogging mama. Upon becoming a mom, Krissy founded B-Inspired Mama simply as a creative outlet, and it ignited a passion within her for blogging and helping fellow moms. Over the past 10 years, between pregnancies and playdates for her children, Sawyer, Priscilla, and J.C., Krissy immersed herself in blogging, social media, and content marketing to grow B-InspiredMama.com into an extensive resource of inspiration for kids' crafts, learning fun, kid-friendly recipes, and creative parenting. Follow her fun via e-mail at B-InspiredMama.com/subscribe and on social media by following @BInspiredMama on Twitter and Instagram, and find her online at Pinterest.com/BInspiredMama, Facebook.com/BInspiredMama, and Facebook.com/SensoryActivitiesForKids.

CPSIA information can be obtained
at www.ICGtesting.com
Printed in the USA
LVHW011323061220
673455LV00007BA/7

9 781641 525381